MY CAPTAIN'S BOOK

STEVEN GERRARD

SECRETS BEHIND THE ARMBAND

Produced by Sport Media, Trinity Mirror North West.

Executive Editor: Ken Rogers. Editor: Steve Hanrahan.
Production Editor: Paul Dove. Art Editor: Rick Cooke.
Sub Editors: Roy Gilfoyle, James Cleary, Michael Haydock.
Designers: Colin Sumpter, Barry Parker, Lee Ashun, Glen Hind,
Alison Gilliland, Jamie Dunmore, James Kenyon, Lisa Critchley, Charles Hearnshaw.
Writers: Chris McLoughlin, David Randles,
Gavin Kirk, John Hynes, Simon Hughes.
Sales and Marketing Manager: Elizabeth Morgan.

With thanks to WMG and Liverpool Football Club.

Published in Great Britain in 2008 by: Trinity Mirror Sport Media,
PO Box 48, Old Hall Street, Liverpool L69 3EB.

Photographs: Trinity Mirror, PA Photos, John Cocks, Colin Sumpter.

Printed by Broad Link Enterprise Ltd.

CONTENTS

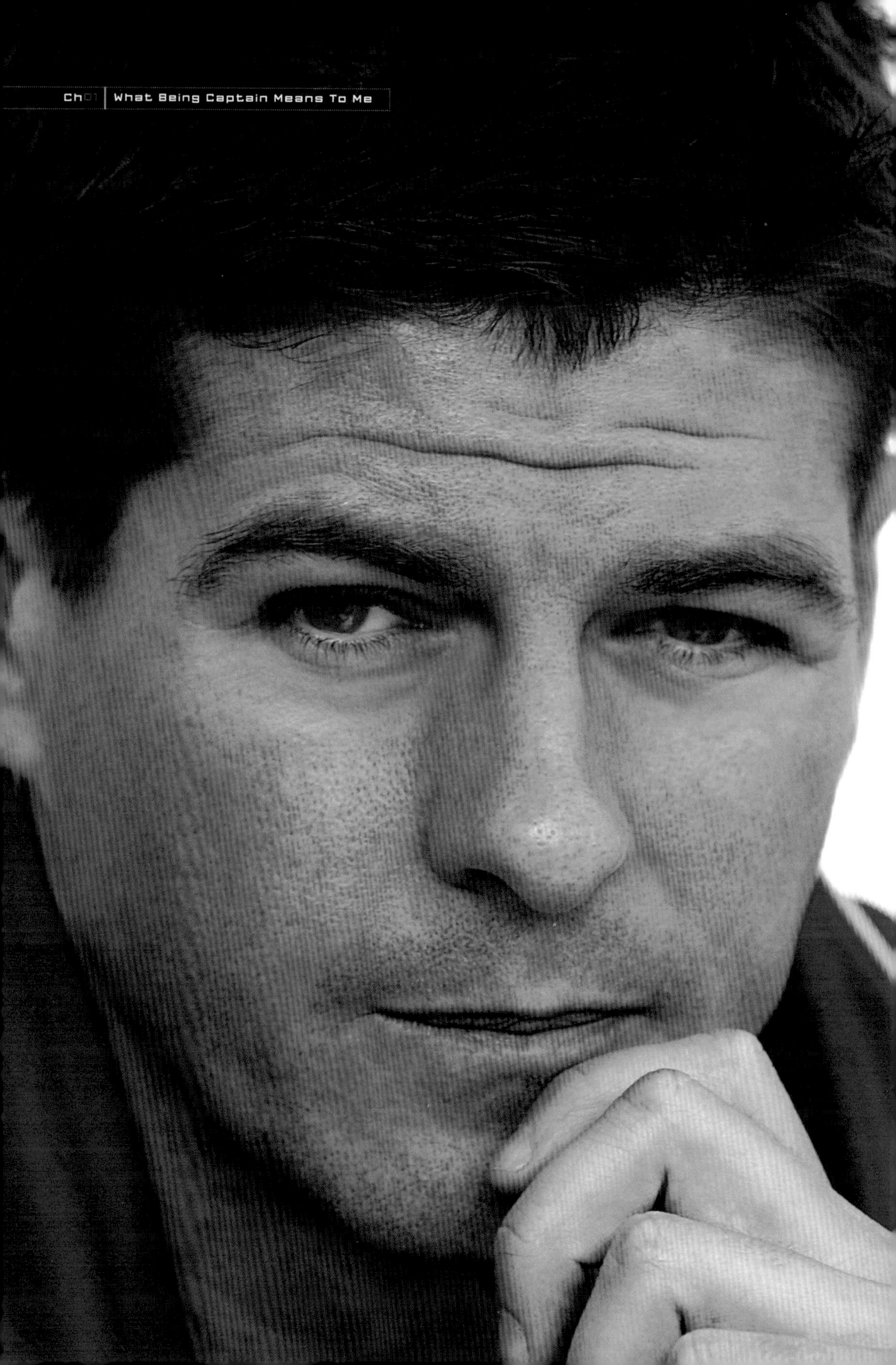

EVERY TIME WE WIN A FOOTBALL MATCH AND I'M WEARING THAT ARMBAND, THE FEELING AND THE BUZZ IS UNBELIEVABLE. AND WHEN YOU LEAD THE TEAM OUT…

Five years on . . .

It's amazing to think that five years have passed since I was first handed the full-time job of being Liverpool captain. I remember when I got my first taste of wearing the armband, in a League Cup tie against Southampton at Anfield in November, 2002. I got to wear it permanently just under a year later.

Someone told me before the Champions League match against Besiktas last season that it was the fifth anniversary of that game against Southampton. I was pleased to reach another landmark and it was a proud moment for me and my family but I honestly couldn't believe that it was five years since that day – it made me feel old!

It really doesn't seem that long ago.

To be honest, I prefer to look forward rather than back. This is an incredibly short playing career and if you spend your time looking back at what you did in the past then you can't be fully concentrated on what you want to do in the future.

I've been lucky in the time that I've been captain of Liverpool because we've enjoyed some real success.

We've been to two Champions League finals and an FA Cup Final, winning two out of three.

I've enjoyed those successes as much as anyone – player or fan. But we want more, we want a hell of a lot more.

As a player at Liverpool FC you are in the business of winning trophies. I want to win every game I play in and every competition that I enter. That's just the way I'm made and the way I was brought up to think about playing for this club.

I'm in a fortunate position in that I'm quite close to some of the most successful players to have represented this club, people like Kenny Dalglish.

That's the message that was drummed into them when they were playing here, that the most important success is the one that's still to come.

That's the way I like to think too. You can't stop at my stage of your career and say to yourself 'look what I've achieved'. I'm 28 now and in my own opinion, I'm far from the finished article as a skipper. There are new things that I still learn every day. I've taken something from every manager I've worked under. It was Gerard Houllier who gave me the captaincy of the club.

I learned under him and now Rafa has helped me become a better captain.

Learning about the armband

I'd say I've learned more from being a captain when things haven't gone too well. You learn more in football from bad experiences really.

Obviously I've had some tremendous highs as captain with the trophies I've lifted.

Every time we win a football match and I'm wearing that armband, the feeling and the buzz is unbelievable.

And when you lead the team out…

These are special feelings that I can only really describe because I've experienced them.

But going out of competitions, bad defeats, losing in cup finals or falling short in the league, you remember and learn from all of that too.

Through different conversations I've had with various coaches throughout those five years, or with different players and other people, I've learned from all of this.

A big responsibility

I think, as captain, I feel more responsible, particularly when we get beat. I'm sure I can speak for Jamie (Carragher) here too. When we get on that bus after a defeat we know there are hundreds of thousands of people around the world who are disappointed and upset that Liverpool lost. But I'd argue to the death that there aren't two people who feel it more than me and Jamie.

I suppose it's because we are captain and vice-captain that we feel this extra responsibility. We're out there and it's in our hands with the rest of the squad. But we are the leaders in the pack.

Three captains

There are different kinds of captains. Where Carra is a shouter, some people say I come across as a quieter captain who leads more by example.

That's easy to say simply because Jamie is so loud. Maybe I'm not as loud as him but that doesn't mean I'm not as vocal as him on the pitch or in the dressing room. It also doesn't mean that he doesn't lead by example just as much as me.

It's all down to different interpretations that form people's opinion, but the main thing is that we've got two captains out there, three if Sami's playing.

The manager asks every player to lead by example. But we are local boys who love the club to death and want nothing but success for it. I think you've got two good captains out there who will do everything we can to make sure the club is doing well.

Enjoy the journey ... so far

T his is my story so far of what it's been like having the massive honour of wearing the captain's armband for the club I've loved all my life. Like I say, I'm 28 now and believe I can still become a better captain from here.

EARLY INSPIRATIONS

Liverpool conquered Europe when I was young.
I was asked to wear the shirts of my heroes again for
a special photo-shoot and I jumped at the chance.

'77
Rome

A totally new experience

I wasn't even born the first time we lifted the European Cup. It would be another two years before I entered the world as another member of a fiercely Red family. But despite that, the glory that was Rome '77 is burned indelibly on my mind. I've watched the video of that amazing night so many times, I sometimes feel as if I played in that game myself.

The sight of Emlyn Hughes lifting that trophy, in that strip, was an inspiring sight for a kid like me who wanted nothing more than to play for the team I loved. I'm so proud to say that I'm now captain, just like Emlyn was then.

I've got a vast collection of football memorabilia but there's just something so special about that 1977 shirt. I just had to see that shirt lying on the table to feel the goose bumps start.

I really enjoyed pulling on the '77 strip again for this photo. As a Liverpool supporter, you know the history behind the strips and you know some of the great names from the past that have worn it. You're wearing something that belongs to legends. That's what they were to me, and still are to me.

It was a very proud moment for me pulling it on,

I was just a bit terrified of doing it damage because of the history attached to it.

As well as my dad sitting me down in front of that video, my old man also told me stories about that great team of Bob Paisley's. He made sure I knew who I was supporting and the reasons why this club is such a unique club. You get that sense from this strip too. Even the kit itself is a classic kit. It's a very striking kit but the materials they use to make them have improved a bit over the years – this one reminds me of my old school kit!

I don't think you can underestimate how important that one victory was to everything that has followed since. We needed a catalyst and that victory in '77 was it.

I've seen the goals so many times. Steve Heighway's pass for Terry McDermott's opener, a great finish into the bottom corner. Moenchengladbach equalising and looking like they'd push on until Ray Clemence made a wonder save.

From that moment we got a new belief. It was a great night for Liverpool players and fans, a totally new experience but one we'd get used to in the coming years.

'I'VE WATCHED THE VIDEO OF THAT AMAZING NIGHT SO MANY TIMES, I SOMETIMES FEEL AS IF I PLAYED IN THAT GAME MYSELF'

Like a home game for us

We know the importance of producing the goods in Europe when the pressure is on and that's what they did in '78, they turned it on when it counted. There were times when they had to win ugly to get through but that's sometimes what you have to do.

It wasn't an easy route to the final either. Moenchengladbach were a great team, one of the most famous at the time, but we out-classed them at Anfield.

I've had to rely on DVDs again and my dad and family for my memories of that game, but I've talked about it a lot with some of the players who played. We had a really scary moment at the end when it looked like the Belgians were going to equalise but the ball was cleared off the line and we went on to win comfortably.

I've been lucky enough to become good friends with Kenny Dalglish over the years and I've chewed his ear off about that night a few times.

He was kind enough to give me one of the last strips he wore for Liverpool before he retired as a player and I've got it in my collection along with the strips I've collected over the years. It's got its own special place.

That night was a special night for all the fans too, because the final was at Wembley.

It was like a home game for us that night because of the number of fans we took.

Nothing's changed either over the years, because the Ataturk Stadium looked exactly the same when the travelling Kop took over the stadium in 2005 – and fortunately the end result was the same too.

'I'VE BEEN LUCKY ENOUGH TO BECOME GOOD FRIENDS WITH KENNY DALGLISH OVER THE YEARS AND I'VE CHEWED HIS EAR OFF ABOUT THAT NIGHT A FEW TIMES'

'81
Paris

The opposite of Istanbul

Our 1-0 victory over Real Madrid in Paris wasn't the best final of the five to watch, and it looked like the game was destined for penalties. That was until Alan Kennedy took it upon himself to win it with less than 10 minutes left with a great solo run and finish.

From what my old man told me I know there was a lot of hype surrounding this game and everyone was expecting a classic final.

It was Liverpool, at the time Europe's dominant team, against Real Madrid who were the specialists at the European Cup.

Both teams had reputations for playing great football at the time and I think everyone thought this was going to be an end to end game with lots of chances. It didn't work out like that.

It was the opposite of our game against AC Milan in 2005. People expected ours to be a cagey final and it turned into a goals feast.

It was quite a tough game. Real had the reputation for good football but they were flying into tackles everywhere on the pitch. The game never really got flowing.

That didn't matter to anyone in the crowd that night in Paris. The moment Alan Kennedy's shot hit the back of the net they knew it was Liverpool's cup for a third time.

I was too young at the time but Alan Kennedy's goal that night was one of those I used to try and copy when I was kicking a ball around with my mates. It was a great strike and the keeper was confused.

He thought the angle was too narrow for Alan to shoot so he starts to go the other way, expecting him to cross it and before he can react it's in the back of his net.

'ALAN KENNEDY'S GOAL THAT NIGHT WAS ONE OF THOSE I USED TO TRY AND COPY WHEN I WAS KICKING A BALL AROUND WITH MY MATES'

'84
Rome

I remember this game clearly

This is one I actually remember because I was a little bit older and it was live on the television.

I remember being excited all day because my dad was telling me the game was coming up and really getting me wound up.

It was a very difficult situation for Liverpool, going to Rome to play against a team from the Italian capital. It should have been like a home game for the Italians but that would be forgetting the numbers our fans travel with.

We know from Istanbul that our fans managed to get their hands on tickets for every part of the stadium and when we ran out for the warm-up it felt like a home game at Anfield because of the noise. It was a bit like that in Rome – the Italians should have had the numbers but I'm not sure they did. It certainly sounded like there were more Liverpool fans in the Stadio Olympico on the television.

I actually remember the game very clearly, but maybe that's got something to do with the number of times I watched it. We got off to the perfect start early on when Phil Neal made the most of an error from the Roma keeper and stuck the ball in the back of the net.

Roma were effectively the home team and had to take the game to us after that early goal and to be fair to them they did it well.

They got level before the interval from a header and probably shaded the second half on possession and chances created. I remember Graeme Souness being immense in midfield though, that's another image that stuck.

With so few chances in extra time, you knew it would be decided on penalties long before the final whistle.

It's important to get off to a good start in a shoot-out but Steve Nicol missed the first one and Roma scored. They must have been sure they had an advantage but then they missed their second kick while Phil Neal scored.

Souness scored again and Roma levelled but Rushie made no mistake and the pressure was really on Roma's next taker. It wasn't a Shevchenko situation where he had to score to stay alive but when he missed, it gave us a free shot for the match. Alan Kennedy made no mistake and we'd won it four times.

I had that kit that we wore in '84 and it was never ever off my back, it might even be lying around somewhere at home now.

'I HAD THAT KIT THAT WE WORE IN '84 AS A KID AND IT WAS NEVER EVER OFF MY BACK'

FIRST LEADERS

I've talked about my early inspirations growing up. But it's not just the likes of Kenny Dalglish, Emlyn Hughes and Phil Thompson that spurred me on as a young player . . .

Learning young: The first armband

The first team I captained was my primary school team. I played two years above my age, up at my brother's age group.

By the time I got to fourth year I'd been playing for the team for a couple of years already so that's probably why I got chosen to be captain. The teacher told the other lads I already had the experience of playing and gave me the captaincy.

That was fourth year primary so I must have been about 10 or 11 at the time. Normally you would only play for the school team in the last year of primary school but I was always playing with my brother and his mates anyway so I was used to it.

I was always trying to play with kids that were older than me. I always wanted to be like my brother, so any game in the street or on the field, most of the lads would be two or three years older than me.

That was a big help at that age. It helped toughen me up and I became more vocal when I was playing with kids of my own age.

I was probably a bit bossy if you like. I suppose I had the makings of a captain in me even at a young age.

This old picture of me as school captain may not be the best quality but it sums up how I was back in those days.

I loved the game with a passion and if I didn't have a ball in my hands then I had one at my feet!

It's fair to say that I was always more interested in the football than the lessons which is why I never did as well at school as I could have done.

They were good days though. I used to love them.

'I WAS PROBABLY A BIT BOSSY. I SUPPOSE I HAD THE MAKINGS OF A CAPTAIN EVEN AT A YOUNG AGE'

My Dad - the captain behind the captain

It's an honour to captain any team. My dad was buzzing when he found out I was captain of the school team.

Straight away he was telling me about all the past captains of Liverpool and what you should do as captain.

Sometimes I'd have a little moan at a few of the kids who maybe didn't have the same ability as me. My dad would pull me aside and tell me that as captain I should be helping those kids.

From an early age I was getting the right pointers and advice from my dad about how to behave and conduct myself as captain of a football team.

He would tell me that he could see me becoming captain of Liverpool one day. It was always a case of him telling me to keep doing what I was doing and one day it would happen.

My ole fella doesn't just see the football side of it. He watches my all round behaviour on the pitch and compares that to how he says a captain should behave. Sometimes he would say to me that I'd played alright in a certain game but that I looked a bit down and my body language wasn't right.

He was over the moon when I told him I was Liverpool captain. He just told me to give it my best shot and that he was sure I'd be good at it.

My dad doesn't give that much away too easily but I could tell by the tone of his voice that he was really pleased for me. But at the same time he was still advising me how to behave and react to the responsibility of being captain.

He still does it to this day. Sometimes I can get a bit down or maybe a bit over-excited but he's always the one who tells me to keep my feet on the ground.

That's what people forget. Sometimes they think that just because you're captain you've automatically got to play well in every game but there's a lot more to it than that. It's about how you act out on the training ground and how I am with people in and around the club, not just my team-mates but everybody on and off the pitch.

Being a captain is not just about how you play. It's all of these other things and more.

'HAVING THE LIKES OF STEVE HEIGHWAY AND THE COACHES AT LIVERPOOL THERE TO PUT AN ARM AROUND MY SHOULDER AND TEACH ME HOW TO BE MORE HELPFUL ON THE PITCH REALLY HELPED MY DEVELOPMENT AS A CAPTAIN'

Teachers and coaches

As well as my dad, I would have my school teachers and the coaches at Liverpool, people like Steve Heighway, guiding me and teaching me about responsibility.

Without wanting to sound too big-headed, I was always good in my own age group.

When you're young, you can sometimes start taking that for granted and getting on other kids' backs who don't share that same ability.

That's wrong and you learn that as you get older. But at the time I might get frustrated because other lads may not see things I did on a pitch or be on the same wavelength.

Having the likes of Steve Heighway and all the coaches at Liverpool there to put an arm around my shoulder and teach me how to be more helpful on the pitch really helped my development as a captain.

Still playing on the streets

ere's a few photos of me from my early days at Liverpool – see if you can recognise me. I've got some great memories.

To be honest, I don't think the way I play the game now and the way I played on the streets as a lad is too different because I have always wanted to win any game of football I play. I realise that a lot of people would give their left arm to be where I am now and that inspires you. I'm a fan myself and

if things had worked out differently for me then I'd have been stood on the Kop with them. I know the levels they demand from the team because it's the same as I demand of myself.

I think the desire to work hard is just the result of where I grew up and comes naturally. No-one can play at their best every week but so long as the fans see people giving everything they've got then I think they will forgive your off-days.

MY DREAM JOB

Gerard Houllier was the manager who first handed me the armband full time. It was October 2003 and a special day in my career that I will never forget. I'll always be grateful for the faith he showed in me and hopefully I have gone on to fulfil his and other people's expectations.

Stevie turned from an Academy player into an international regular for England. At the time, I knew his development was still not finished because I know he was still keen to improve and progress in many areas.

Not only did he enjoy playing and training but he liked practicing all the time to become a better player. That's a very good thing when a player of his ability is determined to keep pushing himself to improve. He does his job in a very committed way.

What I liked about him was the way he always gave 100 per cent in training. I read somewhere once that Paolo Maldini does the same. He's another great captain and that's the mark of a true professional. Steven leads by example in training and it's a great example for all the young players at the club.

I've always said that a manager's job is to help the players progress as footballers on the pitch and men off it. I must stress the fact that Stevie not only progressed as a player but also as a man.

'STEVIE NOT ONLY PROGRESSED AS A PLAYER BUT AS A MAN. THAT'S WHY I MADE HIM CAPTAIN

That's why I made him the Liverpool captain.

I said at the time that we had three leaders in the team – Michael Owen at the front, Sami Hyypia at the back and Steven in the middle.

Stevie became a person that the players wanted to play for and win for. He earned their respect through hard work.

. . . . thanks Gerard!

'I DREAMED WHEN I WAS A BOY THAT I WOULD BE CAPTAIN OF LIVERPOOL SO I WAS DETERMINED TO MAKE THE MOST OF IT WHEN IT CAME'

M y first match as official club captain was against Olimpija Ljubljana. It was a dream come true for me, probably one of the best days of my life. I was buzzing. I always thought it would happen one day because the manager told me that was what he wanted but coming so early and at 23 years of age was a bit of a shock. I was captain of my school side and I used to go along to Anfield and I always looked up to people like John Barnes who captained the team in the '90s. When I first got the job, I said I wanted to do as well as the players who have

captained Liverpool. We've had some great captains at this club – people like Alan Hansen, Phil Thompson, Graeme Souness, John Barnes and hopefully I can keep following in their footsteps. I said at the time that I would give it my best shot and that I thought I would thrive on the responsibility.

I was determined to make the most of it when i came. There was a lot of pressure but even thoug I was young myself, I knew I had to help some of the younger members of the squad. I also had to make sure that my own form was spot on

A victory in my first game

t was a professional performance overall in my first match as official Liverpool captain in the first round, second leg of the UEFA Cup. We cruised through 3-0 in the end. They weren't a bad ide but we got the ball down and played some good stuff.

Not everything went according to plan for me on a personal level though. I was substituted seconds before Liverpool won a penalty . . . that was missed by El-Hadji Diouf. I was on that penalty – I was gutted when I came off!

I remember that we were missing a few players for the game and the two young French lads – Anthony Le Tallec and Florent Sinama-Pongolle – were given a chance. I felt as captain I had to help them on the night but I thought both were magnificent. Le Tallec scored his first goal for the club and Emile Heskey's 50th Reds goal plus a

Harry Kewell effort meant it was a winning start to my captaincy. We slipped to a 1-0 defeat to Portsmouth after that, though, but we were soon back on track with a 3-1 win over Leeds at Anfield, a thrilling 4-3 victory at Ewood Park and a 2-1 win at Fulham. I was up and running as captain of the team I loved.

'I WAS SUBSTITUTED MINUTES BEFORE LIVERPOOL WON A PENALTY . . . WHICH WAS MISSED BY EL-HADJI DIOUF'

On Sami . . .

It was Sami who handed me the armband. As you'd expect from such an honest professional – and an Anfield legend – he was a man about the situation. He said I deserved it and that if I needed any help I could go to him and get it. I've always had a good relationship with him and that didn't change. Sami was brilliant against Ljubljana. He played with a weight off his shoulders because he had been under a fair bit of pressure.

On a 'downer' after getting the armband

So getting the armband was great but because I took the captaincy off Sami, it was also something of a strange feeling when it happened. I'd always wanted to be the captain of Liverpool from a young age, from about 14 or 15.

But I didn't want to get it how I eventually did. I didn't want to take it from someone. I didn't want it as a consequence of someone else having to give the captaincy up, as was the case when I took over from Sami.

I'd rather someone would have retired and it was passed on, or maybe if they'd given it up themselves and the next in line got it.

As it happened it was taken off one of my good friends. It was a bit uncomfortable for me in that sense as I didn't know how he was going to react.

I was actually a bit down about receiving the captaincy in that way. When I got the captaincy, I made a phone call to my dad and he was over the moon.

But one of the first things he said to me was to make sure I spoke to Sami about it. He told me he was made up for me and that I deserved it but was also conscious of Sami's feelings.

Obviously, time is a good healer and. as I say, Sami was great over it. He was a top professional about it all and wished me all the best, telling me that if I ever needed any help or advice he was always there for me.

I've bounced off Sami ever since, and Carra. Those two have helped me tremendously along the way.

Sami's reaction summed him up. He was obviously upset and gutted at the fact he had to give the armband up but he kept those feelings inside, to himself. As always, he was the true professional and said the right things at the right time.

He approached me man to man and was certainly a man himself about it.

'SAMI WAS GREAT OVER IT. HE WAS A TOP PROFESSIONAL ABOUT IT ALL AND WISHED ME ALL THE BEST. I'VE BOUNCED OFF SAMI EVER SINCE'

What Sami said . . .

Of course I am not happy about it (losing the captaincy) but I feel relief now that I can get used to the idea.

I don't feel myself a worse player because I don't have the armband anymore. There was nothing dramatic over changing the captaincy. I didn't say anything because it was the manager's decision and I respect that. Being captain in England is not an easy job because it demands a lot from you, even outside the ground. I am the same lad whether I have the armband or not.

I believe that captaincy will bring Steven to a new level. He's a young and talented English player who has a great future ahead of him. He's a great lad on and off the pitch.

PRE-MATCH ROUTINE

Preparing for a game is vitally important – physically and mentally. If you're not feeling right yourself, then you won't be able to lead the team in the way that you would like.

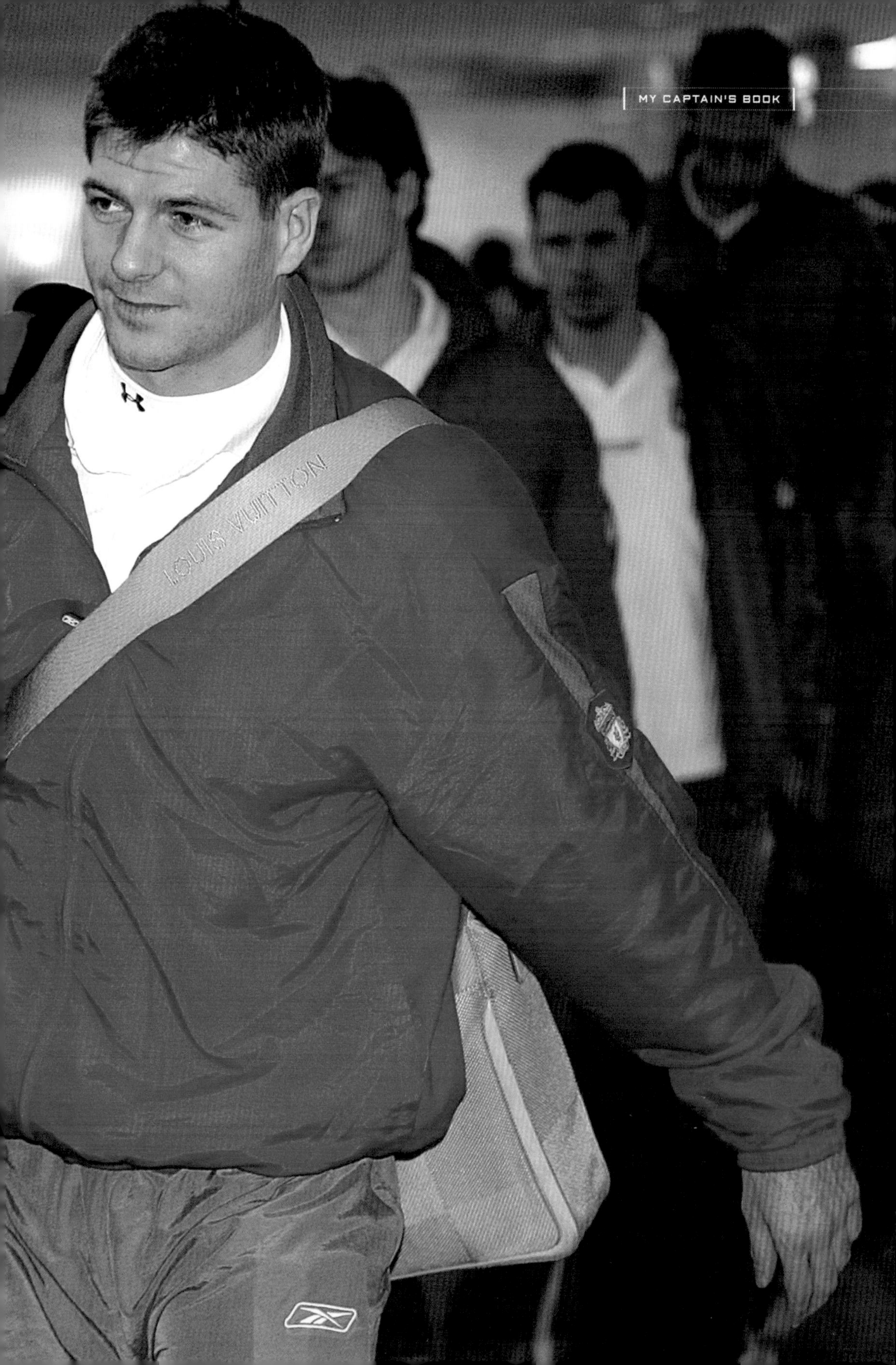
LOUIS VUITTON

Rituals

There are different rituals for home and away games when the various timescales can influence how and when you do certain things.

Then there are certain things that you try to do the same before every game, home or away. The main one is make sure I sleep well, not just the night before a game but in the days leading up to it. With that I also make sure I eat all the right foods. They are the two main things preparation wise that I like to get right before I go out on the pitch.

Superstitions

I make sure I always do things in the same order before a game.
I get to the ground, have a little nose at the programme, then I'll get out of my suit as soon as I can if I'm wearing one.

I've never liked wearing suits and always found them uncomfortable. It's always nice to get into the kit. Once I'm in the dressing room, I've already thought the game through in my head many times either in the hotel room or in my house.

Inside the captain's locker

I don't carry loads of personal items around with me when I'm getting ready for a game. It's just simple stuff. The staff at Liverpool will ensure that we've got everything we need.

Inside my locker I've got some old trophies and things like that which I may have picked up over the years that are still in there for no other reason other than I just haven't got round to taking them home yet.

We have lockers at Melwood but there's nothing really from a captain's point of view that I keep in there.

'I'D SAY 70-80 PER CENT OF THE PLAYERS GET CHANGED IN THE SAME PLACE'

Sitting in the same place

At Anfield I'll always get changed in the same place. There are no numbers on spaces but the kit man will know where I want my kit laying out before every game.

I'd say 70-80 per cent of the players get changed in the same place before every match. I'm not really superstitious but I suppose you could call it that in this case.

I just like to sit and get ready in the same place. Since I've been sitting there we've won the Champions League and the FA Cup. You just do the same things and have the same routine.

If you moved place and then had a nightmare on the pitch you'd be thinking about having changed your routine.

'I'LL THINK ABOUT WHO I'M UP AGAINST PERSONALLY AND WHO THE TEAM ARE UP AGAINST AS A COLLECTIVE'

Focus on the game

By this time I'm just focusing on the game and nothing else is going through my mind. I'll think about who I'm up against personally as well as who the team are up against as a collective.

I'll also think about what the manager and the coaching staff have drilled into us in the days leading up to the game.

These are the things going through my mind. What have I been told to do? What have we been told to do as a team?

Helping others

On top of all of this before a game are the responsibilities as a captain. What have I got to do to help the other players around the dressing room?

If there's any of the younger lads in there it may be a big game for them but one I've played hundreds of.

I may know what I've got to do but I can see on their faces that they may be a bit nervous. If that's the case I'll go over and help them and make sure everyone's prepared.

It's a case of basically making sure nobody's going to have any regrets when they come off the pitch.

I've come off pitches before when maybe we haven't got the result we've wanted and I've thought to myself that maybe I haven't looked at the set-pieces for them enough.

Or other players may be feeling like they haven't played as well as they would have liked and I'll think to myself 'I could have helped him a bit more during or before that game.'

INSIDE THE DRESSING ROOM

The dressing room is at the heart of Anfield. It's where we plan our battles and focus on the challenges that lie ahead of us as a team.

Sitting next to Sami

I've sat next to Sami Hyypia since we've both been here really. When I first broke into the squad I sat wherever I was put but since I became a permanent fixture in the team Sami has always been to the right of me.

The player to the left of me has always changed though. It was Emile Heskey, then El Hadji Diouf. Then it was Djibril Cisse and now Ryan Babel.

I don't know if any other captains once sat where I sit now. There's a lot of history and heritage in that dressing room but I don't know who used to sit where.

Sticking together

The home dressing room is smaller than the away one at Anfield. People often ask why we don't use the larger dressing room but it's good to be closer together, more tight knit if you like, before we go out.

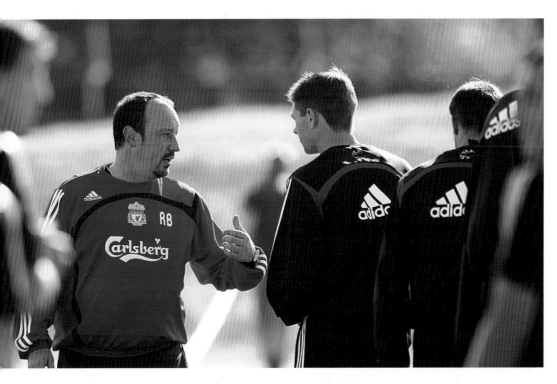

'YOU HAVE TO BE AWARE THAT THE MANAGER IS THE BOSS OF THE DRESSING ROOM. THE CAPTAIN IS NOT THE MOST IMPORTANT FIGURE'

The boss of the dressing room

Everyone has their own dressing room routine or ritual if you like.

You have to be aware of that but also as captain you have to be aware that the manager is the boss of the dressing room. The captain is not the most important figure in there.

The manager will bring the captain in if he feels he needs the captain to say anything.

But most of my captain's work in the dressing room will be on a one on one basis with each player rather than sit with the whole team listening as a group to what I have to say.

Talking about the game

There is always a lot of vocal stuff going on anyway leading up to the game itself. We'll have various players geeing each other up and making sure everyone's prepared.

Players will also talk to each other individually to make sure they all know what they have to do.

For example, if you're playing right midfield you might speak to the right back to make sure you're both spot on with what you have to do.

There's a lot of chit-chat and conversations being exchanged in the hour or so before a game.

Dressing room chats - and the huddle

I don't really give group pep talks, like I say. Sometimes under both Houllier and Benitez I've gone ahead and given a pep talk but it's not really my style to do that unless I'm asked to.

You've also probably seen us on the pitch when we gather in a huddle before games. I may speak as captain then or the vice-captain may say something.

Other times we will also nominate another player to speak just to make sure everyone's ready for it.

Sometimes you'll get quieter people in the squad and you're not always sure what they're thinking. It's good to test them at times to see how much they're up for it too.

The feeling and response you get from giving that little talk before a game is good. You're glad you've done it and get a buzz from it. I've done it quite a few times but it's good to pass that on to the other lads every now and again as well.

The majority of the time I'll do my captain stuff on a one on one basis around the dressing room and speak to people individually.

It's about the team

I've been asked about what I do at half-time: If someone has had a bit of a nightmare in the first half, would I pull them to one side and have a word, try to sort their head out.

Sometimes that happens but you've got to work that player out as an individual. You need to know what they respond to. Some players need a kick up the arse; I do myself sometimes. Other players need a quiet chat or more of a confidence boost.

You can have a top player whose confidence may be low or the crowd can affect certain players.

As captain you have to get the balance right and work out how to approach a player. If a player's confidence is low it's pointless going in and having a go at him.

It may be better to go and sit next to him and put your arm around him and say 'look, that didn't go as well as it could have done but there's another 45 minutes there. You know you're capable of turning it around and we can win the game.'

That's the most important thing you learn as a captain. It's about the team.

You do what you feel you need to help the team get the right result. That's what's always going through my mind.

> ## 'JOHN PUT SEVEN YEARS' GOOD SERVICE IN AT THIS CLUB. HE DIDN'T MEAN TO SCORE THE OWN GOAL, IT JUST HAPPENED AND COULD HAVE HAPPENED TO ANY ONE OF US'

Captain - and being a good mate

Immediately after John Arne Riise scored 'that' own goal against Chelsea in the Champions League semi-final at Anfield, I made sure I backed him in the press afterwards.

Obviously, we were all aware that that own goal could be vital. With hindsight we now know it was probably the difference between us going out or progressing to the final.

But this was a lad we're all good friends with. Myself and people like Carra had played with John for seven years.

At the same time we were also aware he would be leaving at the end of the season. That might have made it easy for the likes of me and Jamie to blame John and say it was all his fault.

But that was the wrong way to go about it. The right way was just to admit he'd made a mistake and say 'it's happened now, let's all move on.'

John put seven years' good service in at this club. He didn't mean to score the own goal, it just happened and could have happened to any one of us. I know what it's like having scored one myself in a final against Chelsea.

In that case it wasn't really about being a captain, it was just about being a good mate for him and reminding people what a good servant he had been to the club.

On my way

From the dressing room, it's into the tunnel where I'll run through some final thoughts in my head about the game. I always touch the 'This is Anfield' sign on my way out.

TUNNEL VISION

I like to get into the tunnel and just think about that game, nothing else. It's not good if you're in the tunnel and you've maybe got little things going on off the pitch or you're concerned about something going into the game that you're not really sure about. I like to know exactly what I've got to do and have my mind totally focused on the game. It's a sign of respect to shake hands with the other captain and maybe with the officials. But you won't see me turning round talking to anyone as it can take away from the focus.

Beware mascots!

The one time you may have seen me afford a smile in the tunnel was at Chelsea when the mascot played a trick on me.

I went to shake hands with him and he drew his hand away and pulled a face at me. If it was an adult who tried it I probably would have wanted to wring their neck! But because it was a kid and how it happened I saw the funny side.

We've all been kids and he had me off. He deserved a smile and a little pat on the head and that was it. I know John Terry wasn't happy about it as the home captain and, to be fair, I wouldn't want it to happen to another captain at Anfield – not just as we're waiting to go out. But it was just a kid and I saw the funny side of it.

Following in legends' footsteps

Many times I've thought about the previous captains who've walked that same route from the tunnel on to the pitch, leading the team out. Emlyn Hughes, Phil Neal, Alan Hansen, so many great Liverpool players and captains. Some of them will have their say in this book later on.

I also think back to people, other captains, who have helped me along the way. Someone like Phil Thompson who even to this day I'm still in touch with.

He's a man who captained the club who I've got an awful lot of respect for. He's always helped me both on and off the pitch, how to be a better person and how to go about certain issues. He's someone who even to this day I can bounce off for advice if I need it.

He's done it all. He's been a good player as well as a good captain. He's been assistant manager, managed the club, even managed the reserves.

He knows how the club works but, importantly, knows exactly how a captain should behave on and off the pitch.

He's experienced it himself so who better to listen to and get help from. If a successful captain of this club says you should do this or you should do that he's going to be right and you tend to sit up and listen.

THE TOSS

One aspect of my captain's role is the toss before the game. I've been asked whether or not I make the same call – heads or tails. The truth is that I vary it. Sometimes I'll make the call simply depending on which way the coin is facing in the referee's hand before he tosses it. Sometimes I'll go the opposite of what I can see before it gets flicked. I don't know why I do that, I just do.

A winning ratio

I'm not sure what my ratio is at Anfield but I'm pretty happy with it. When we're at Anfield I'd say the majority of teams – other captains – try to turn us around so we're attacking the Kop in the first half. I'd say about 90 per cent of them try to do it. Maybe they're under orders from their managers to do it.

It's quite an important thing at Anfield because a lot of breakthroughs against teams don't come until the second half when we're usually attacking the Kop.

We seem to be playing in to the Kop a lot in the second half so I must be winning quite a few tosses in that sense.

I'm pretty happy with my success rate. Obviously I've lost a few which I've been a bit upset over but it's been quite good for me at Anfield.

It can be just as important at some away grounds too, where I might be thinking we want to be kicking into our fans second half because they pull us into them.

'I'M PRETTY HAPPY WITH MY SUCCESS RATE. OBVIOUSLY I'VE LOST A FEW WHICH I'VE BEEN A BIT UPSET OVER BUT IT'S BEEN QUITE GOOD FOR ME AT ANFIELD'

Taking other players' advice

Sometimes players will come up to me, say Pepe Reina for example, because of an issue with the sun. Pepe might say to me 'we can't kick that way first half because the sun is too bright. You've got to win the toss and change us round'.

If you're defending high balls into the sun it can cause mayhem so I'll always try and change us round in those situations.

As a goalkeeper the last thing Pepe wants is the sun in his eyes.

The chances are it will be lower for the second half or the weather could even change so it's best to minimize the problem if possible.

LEADING BY EXAMPLE

All captains are different and there is no right or wrong when it comes to style of leadership. One thing's for certain, though. You have to be seen to be doing the right things yourself, otherwise other players won't respect you in the way that you want. Here's a few personal qualities that I've learned you need if you want to be a successful player at the top level – and a successful captain that others can look up to.

Growing pains and working on fitness

Years ago I had absolutely no confidence in my body being able to play 50 or 60 games a season. It really used to get me down and there were times when, naturally, you wonder whether you'll ever be able to stay fit long enough to become a regular. Those days now are thankfully long gone.

In the past four or five years, everything's come together for me, and I feel great. You are always wary of getting carried away, but I train every day the same as the rest of the lads and it's very, very rare for me to ever miss a session. That simply wasn't the way it used to be.

I've worked hard to get to where I am today, but I owe a massive debt of thanks to the doctor and the physios and other medics at the football club for getting my body to where it is now.

I just didn't think it was possible because of the problems I had with my body when I was growing up. It was an incredibly frustrating time for me and every time I felt I was starting to get back to full fitness I would break down again.

Now I'm playing every season and I feel great. The last real lay-off I had was after breaking a metatarsal at Old Trafford and that led to quite a long lay-off for me. That's just one of those things that happens in football though and it came from going over on my foot – there wasn't even anybody near me when it happened. But I got back from that quickly and played out the rest of the 2005 season – and it ended quite well for us!

I've got a routine that I've got to follow before and after games and in the week at Melwood but to be very honest I'm terrible with it

I've got to do a special programme in the gym during the week and I hate it. The physios have got to drag me in to do it – but they've got to find me first.

I know it's important and I know it's helped me get to this point, keeping me at the level I'm at in the game but it's repetitive and I'll never enjoy it. But as long as there's a benefit there I'll keep at it.

Be honest with yourself

I think it's always important to be honest with yourself. If you can't deal with your own game then you'll have no chance of helping others to deal with situations in theirs. I'm my own worst critic and I know when I've played well and when I've not.

If you've not performed to your highest level then you have to admit that. Then team-mates can see that you are demanding the best from yourself.

I've been named in the PFA Team of the Year on a couple of occasions and I must admit that I was even embarrassed to be in there on one occasion because I simply felt that I didn't deserve to be in there. When that happens, I take no pride from the fact that my name's on the list. Especially when there could be people at my own club that should be in there ahead of me.

'IF YOU'VE NOT PERFORMED TO YOUR HIGHEST LEVEL THEN YOU HAVE TO ADMIT THAT. THEN TEAM-MATES CAN SEE THAT YOU ARE DEMANDING THE BEST FROM YOURSELF'

Dealing with criticism

When things aren't going well on the pitch, : I don't think the right thing to do is hide yourself away. It would be the easiest thing in the world for me to go home to my house and shut myself away, avoid the papers and websites and just pretend it's not happening but that's not the kind of person I am.

I take it on the chin. When we won the European Cup and the FA Cup I enjoyed going out in the city and meeting the fans and seeing them enjoy our success and I'll still do the same when we're having a hard time. I can't say I enjoy meeting the punters but they've got every right to be disappointed. They are paying their hard earned money to come and watch us across the country and they're entitled to their opinion. You can't take the acclaim when things go your way if you're not prepared for the opposite when things don't go for you. I don't mind criticism if it's constructive, I'll take it on the chin until we turn things around. And we will always turn things around.

I read the fanzines and I read the messageboards at home, and some of them are a lot better than others and some of the criticism of us is entirely justified. We expect it and it's there. But we know people still have faith in us and people still believe in us.

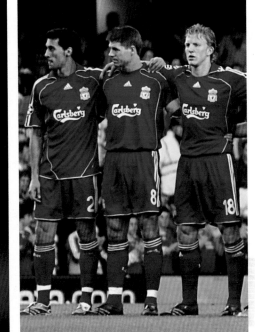

A question of trust

The way I see it, any team – and at Liverpool it's no different – is going to come up against adversity during the course of a season. We will encounter things that are really going to test us as a group. If we don't trust each other and believe in each other then it's going to be hard to be successful. You need relationships to be spot on to conquer them.

Conquering nerves

Personally, in the Champions League final in Istanbul, everything was new for me and it took its toll. Everyone was talking about the history this club has in the European Cup and our previous successes and we felt a bit of pressure on us to emulate some of their achievements.

I know I wasted a lot of energy with nerves before the game but I won't make the same mistakes again. I can't speak for the rest of the boys from 2005 but I'm sure they felt the same pressures as me and it had the same effect on them.

When you're nervous you get tight, you don't make the right decisions and you don't play to the best of your ability. Having a few nerves are important before the game, but we had too much in the team in 2005 and I think it probably showed in the first 45 minutes. It was only really when we were staring down the barrel of the gun at half-time that we started to play anything like ourselves.

We didn't do ourselves justice in the first half in Istanbul. The comeback was incredible, something no-one who was there, or saw it on TV will ever forget, but we shouldn't have been in that position in the first place. We were a better side in 2005 than we showed on the night.

Mind games

As a player, you have to deal with the psychological side of the game – and that's even more important when you're skipper of the team. There are players that can play mind games and try to put you off your game. AC Milan's Gennaro Gattuso has tried. He's got a few tricks up his sleeve and he looks to do things that a lot of other midfield players in the world don't do.

He tries to get in your head and psyche you out before and during games but you've just got to ignore that and concentrate on your own game. Those kind of mind games and ploys don't interest me, they certainly don't have any affect on how I play.

Setting the standards . . . and hard work

I've spoken about how you have to be honest with yourself. The only way that can happen is by taking responsibility for yourself and your performances. Going away from games, going home at night and looking at the league table I think you have to realise that you're not doing your job properly if Liverpool are in a bad position.

The team can't function unless individuals are functioning fully. That's the first thing. I have to sort my own form out and there are other players in our dressing room who have to do the same as me. I'm sure we'll see better team performances if that happens but we've got to continue to keep doing the right things, keep working hard in training and keep working hard in games.

You don't get anything in football, or any walk of life, without hard work and we've got to remember that. Our success under Rafa Benitez has been built on it, and that's the only way we'll be successful in the future. The difficult thing for me is that I've set standards for myself where people expect top, top performances from me week-in and week-out. That's good, I'd rather play with that type of expectation around me, than not, but when I fall a little bit below that standard people are very quick to notice it, and point it out.

If it's not happening then you don't go home and stand in front of a mirror and pull your hair out. That doesn't help. You watch your games on the television, I always record them for that reason, and you see where you're going wrong. Those are the only ways I know to put things right.

I've been lucky enough to have had quite a few special occasions at this football club while wearing the armband. I was asked to name some favourites and I had no problem in doing that. In fact, I could have picked a few more. Here's my eight to remember. No prizes for guessing what my number one is, though.

8 CAPTAIN'S MOMENTS

V ARSENAL Anfield, Champions League, 08.04.08

That night against Arsenal at Anfield was one of those games that is now going to sit alongside the matches against Chelsea in the semi-finals of the Champions League, and nights like St Etienne from the past.

We got ourselves into trouble a couple of times during the 90 minutes but we had the ability, and more importantly the belief to fight back twice.

Lesser teams would have folded at 2-2. It could have been a hammer blow to our hopes of making it through to the last four in the European Cup. I'm sure you could see what we saw from the stands or from the comfort of the pub or the front room that Arsenal had been reignited by Adebayor's goal.

The manager picked the starting 11 because he was confident we would do what was needed, but he also had a great bench with impact players.

I don't know if he knew the impact Ryan Babel would have against a tiring defence, but with Rafa Benitez nothing would surprise me.

That performance has got to put him up there alongside David Fairclough. We've since tried to get Ryan to dye his hair ginger to complete the look but he's not having it!

I didn't have my best night in a Liverpool shirt, but it was not a night for individuals. It was a night where every single person stood up to be counted against Arsenal. We won the personal battles when we needed to and the chips were down but everyone went the extra yard for their team-mates.

Personally, I was confident from the moment the ref pointed to the spot that I would score.

There were no second chances, and I was delighted to see it hit the back of the net.

If you go high into the corner and hard then it's going to take a wonder save from the keeper to stop it and although Manuel Almunia guessed the right way he couldn't get close to it.

Three semi-finals in four years isn't a bad record to have.

We had the belief

Nou Camp, Champions League, 21.02.07

was very young and inexperienced on the first occasion we went to the Nou Camp. I was just excited to be in that great stadium playing against a great side like Barcelona. I was a bit over-awed by it all and I never really got involved in the game. If I'm being honest, it just passed me by.

This time around I was more experienced, there was more responsibility on me as the captain and I couldn't let the same thing happen. It was great to get the 2-1 win and fitting that Craig Bellamy and John Arne Riise got on the scoresheet. I know what to expect from those kind of games now.

This time around I
was more experienced. I
knew what to expect

V CHELSEA Old Trafford, FA Cup, 22.04.06

The FA Cup semi-final win over Chelsea was a magnificent result, and as far as I'm concerned one which we totally deserved. For 65 or 70 minutes we played as well as we had anywhere that season. It was a pity we didn't go on and make the scoreline more emphatic – but we'd have settled for 2-1 before the game.

We came up against a top class side and beat them well

I'd never played in the San Siro and I relished the chance to do so. I hadn't done it, and it was another one to tick off my list.

Fans like going to famous grounds to watch us and as a player I want to play in the cathedrals around Europe.

I think you could see what the result meant to all of us; players, the manager and the fans.

I don't think that anyone could argue that we didn't deserve to win because we came up against a top class side and beat them well. It wasn't down to luck, it was down to having the right tactics, the right belief in ourselves and the right players.

That was Carra's 100th European game and I don't think he's had too many better nights than that. And then with Fernando up there we've got someone who only needs one chance to score. We were always confident we could nick the goal and that's what happened. He made it almost out of nothing, although Fabio's pass was a great pick.

V MAN UTD Anfield, FA Cup, 18.02.06

It's always a massive game when we play Manchester United and you're sure of a passionate atmosphere whenever they come to Anfield. That was certainly the case when we played them in the FA Cup on the way to Cardiff in 2006. I know the fans really enjoyed that result – beating them 1-0 thanks to Crouchie's header.

I also remember that Didi Hamann was brilliant in that game. It can be difficult when you're not in the team every week and you're playing bits and pieces of games but Didi was such a clever player for us and he didn't disappoint.

You knew exactly what you would get off Didi. His experience meant that if he was not playing for three or four games, he could still come back and know exactly what to do and give you a big performance.

He was my man-of the-match in that game against United and that showed he was a big game player. This is someone who had played in the World Cup final, remember, and it was a big bonus for us to have someone of his experience around. Speaking personally, I've learnt an awful lot from him over the years.

It wasn't just having him in the squad as a player, but he was – and is – a great person too. Every one of us in the midfield learned a lot from Didi.

Beating United . . .

V CHELSEA Anfield, Champions League, 03.05.05

Before Istanbul, I said that this was the best night of my life – by a million miles! The ground was shaking 50 minutes before the game when we were warming up and I have never known anything like it. At the end I felt like jumping in and celebrating with the fans.

Jamie Carragher and Sami Hyypia deserved most of the credit, they were outstanding at the heart of our defence. This was the first time we had beaten Chelsea – who were the Premiership champions – in five games. But this was worth the wait. We beat them again two years later, which was another fantastic night.

The ground was shaking 50 minutes before kick-off

When you're down, it's not over until the end

V WEST HAM Millennium Stadium, FA Cup Final, 13.05.06

I think we learnt a lot from the Milan game a year earlier. When you are down, however you are playing, you know it's not over until the end. We made hard work of it and they played really well. It seems we have to do it the hard way in these finals.

When there are only a couple of minutes left you are fearing the worst.

But that is what drives you on. It was really hot on the day and we were going down with cramp all over the place just like in Istanbul. It was a tough game.

For my first goal, it just sat up really nice to volley it. For my second, I had a bit of luck in there as well. I don't tend to get two goals in a game very often.

Just before the second one I had taken a free-kick and it nearly went out of the stadium so I was delighted to hit the next one like that. I didn't mean to put it exactly there but knew if I got good contact it would hit the target and I caught it really sweetly.

I did not hear the stadium announcer say how much extra time was being added but I knew there wasn't long left and it was really hard – I was all over the place.

Bringing 01 Big Ears home for keeps

V AC MILAN Istanbul, Champions League Final, 25.05.05

This was the greatest night of my life. I thought it was going to be impossible at half-time. I thought it was going to be tears and frustration at the end but we got our belief back with that early goal. They dominated the first half and deserved to be three goals up.

There were a lot of heads down at half-time but the manager changed a few things and we got the early goal we needed. We just had to try and get back in the game in the second half and make it respectable for our fans. We were a different team in the second half. We had been outclassed in the first but were much better in the second, running on empty in extra time and to be honest we were playing for penalties by the end. We were underdogs from the start but we were never beaten.

The fans had saved up for weeks and months to be here, as I knew from my own family and friends. We only had 20,000 tickets officially but there seemed to be a lot more inside the stadium. They were crazy, they were and still are our 12th Man. I dedicate this victory to them.

BOUNCING BACK

You shouldn't be in football – and definitely not a captain – if you can't deal with disappointments. We've had plenty of good times at Liverpool Football Club but there's been some dark days that we've had to contend with too. That's when you look around you and find out who's got the character needed to play for a top club to help us get things back on track. Needless to say, as skipper you have to set an example.

I couldn't believe it - but I hadn't given up on trophy dream

When you think of playing Chelsea in 2005, it's natural to think of that amazing Champions League semi-final. But you may also remember that we played Jose Mourinho's men earlier that season in another big game – the Carling Cup final at Cardiff.

We were winning that game 1-0 thanks to a first minute John Arne Riise strike – and holding out for the victory – before the ball skimmed off the top of my head and in our own goal. That gave Chelsea a late equaliser and as we all know, they went on to win the match in extra time.

We were gutted to lose but that defeat gave me the extra motivation I needed to make sure we lifted a trophy in 2004-05.

That Carling Cup would have been my first trophy as official club captain – something I'd dreamed about doing all my life. I watched the great captains of the past lifting trophies during the real glory years. I had all the videos and as I've already said, I watched them over and over when I was a kid. I really wanted to add a new chapter to the club's history. If we'd held out for the win it would have been the biggest thing to happen to me in football.

I said before the game that it would either be the best day or the worst day of my life. It was the worst. It was a freak goal but it turned the game Chelsea's way. I tried to stretch for it as far as I could but there was nothing I could do. I'd never scored an own goal in my life and now I'd done it in a cup final. I couldn't believe it.

But I hadn't given up the dream of lifting a trophy as skipper of Liverpool and I was rewarded with that amazing night in Istanbul just a few months later. The pain of that Carling Cup final own goal was one of the things that gave me the strength to succeed.

Learning not to see red against the Blues

Mersey derbies are always massive games for me. I'm always pumped up when we meet Everton as I know how much local pride is at stake. But sometimes you can be too wound up. I look back on the game at Anfield in March 2006. I was booked early on for a tackle on Kevin Kilbane and then when I kicked the ball away, referee Phil Dowd saw fit to send me off. That was only in the 18th minute and I'd left the lads a man down with more than an hour left to play. It was stupid of me. The boys did brilliantly to recover from that and get a 3-1 win – but I knew afterwards that I didn't play any part in it. I felt as if I owed myself, the fans and the players a big performance and I made sure that I didn't let them down when the next derby came around.

'IT WAS STUPID OF ME. THE BOYS DID BRILLIANTLY TO RECOVER ... BUT I KNEW AFTER THAT I DIDN'T PLAY ANY PART IN IT'

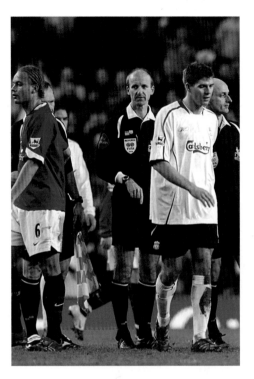

... but you can't hide your emotions

Walking off at Old Trafford, beaten by United and having let the supporters and ourselves down, and watching United fans celebrating their result, hurts me and will always hurt me. I'm the Liverpool captain and a Liverpool fan. It's not a time for me to be smiling, or chatting to United players, because I'm hurting like hell. There's no worse feeling for me than sitting on that team coach replaying a defeat in my head. When that happens, you want another game to play. The best remedy for feeling like that is to get winning – and get winning quickly.

The finals I have lost make me stronger

Losing the Champions League final in 2007 was the complete opposite to what happened in Istanbul.

We had to take it on the chin, move on and try to pick ourselves up. But at the time it was heartbreaking. It was one of the lowest points of my career so far but as I've said, it's how you bounce back from setbacks that counts.

The finals I have lost in my career have made me stronger as a person. Before the game, you know that if you win you will be on top of the world and if you lose you'll be right down at the bottom. When you lose a game like that, you have to use your negative energy in the right way.

I said at the time that we don't want the pain of being losers again. It's not a nice feeling watching someone else take the glory and it's not something we want to get into the habit of.

Don't dwell on what you can't change

I just don't think it was meant to be for us in 2008 when we came up against Chelsea yet again in the Champions League semi-final. I don't think Chelsea were a better team than us in either game. We held our own down there – we did better than that really – but we could have taken one of the chances we created and really cranked up the pressure on them.

But it's gone now.

There's no point dwelling on things that you can't change. If you keep replaying the game in your head over and over again, wondering how you might have done things differently, then you're going to go nuts.

When we reported back for pre-season training in July we remembered how we felt after that second leg. We can use the negatives to our advantage by using them as an inspiration.

WHEN YOU MAKE A MISTAKE YOU HAVE TO PUT IT TO THE BACK OF YOUR MIND AND MOVE ON. THERE'S ALWAYS A LOT, A HELL OF A LOT LEFT TO PLAY FOR . . .

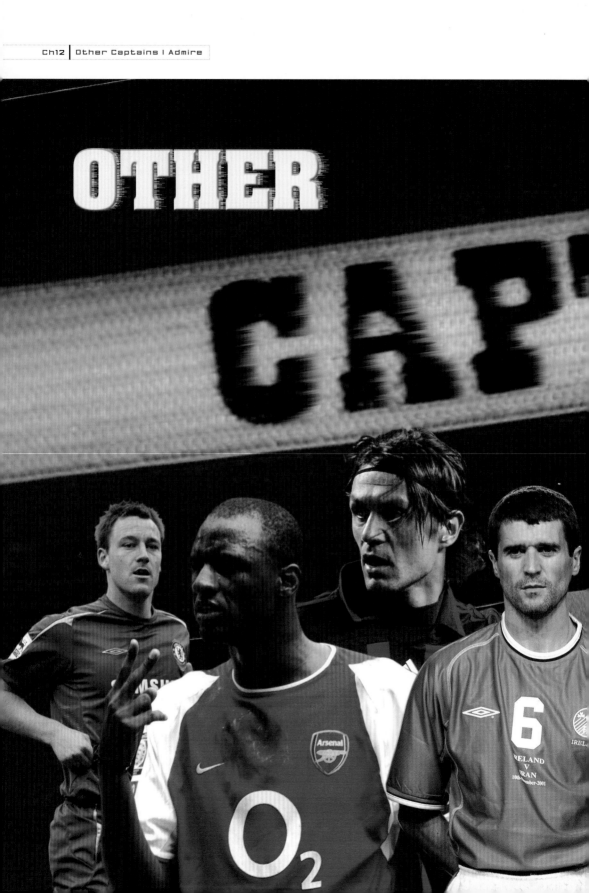

OTHER

CAP

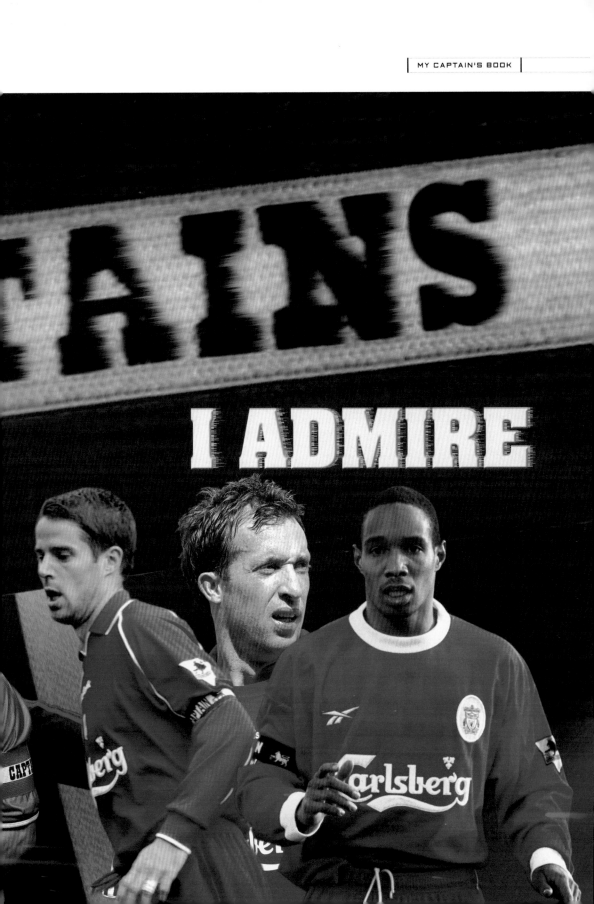

Roy Keane and Patrick Vieira

I know he played for Man United but Roy Keane was a good captain. As far as learning from a captain, for the good and the bad, I probably looked to him and some of the things he did.

Keane and Patrick Vieira were the two main captains when I arrived on the scene and as it happens, they were two players who I always seemed to do well against.

I was very young when I first played against those two, probably about 22 or 23. They were top players in their prime then. They had a big advantage over me at that time, were a lot stronger than me and had so much more experience. But I felt I held my own.

That experience helps me now when I come up against younger players who want to play well against me.

I used to be itching to prove myself against players like that because they were the best around at that time. These young 19 and 20-year - old kids that come up against me now, I know just how much they want to kill me basically.

I have to prepare myself against that to make sure I come out on top.

As a captain, you sometimes have to contend with this as well as leading the team. But that's the way I like it. I like the challenge of other people trying to get the better of me on a football pitch.

Paolo Maldini

It was one of the proudest moments of my life leading the lads out alongside Paolo Maldini in Istanbul. He's one of the best that's ever played the game. But I remember thinking that 'he's won this competition before so he doesn't need another winners' medal'. That's how it worked out – but he had to go and get his own back two years later didn't he!

John Terry

John Terry is someone who I've come up against a few times in recent seasons. He's a good leader on the pitch and someone who conducts himself in the right way. When we beat Chelsea in the Champions League semi-final in 2005, you had to admire his sportsmanship. He must have been devastated but he came and spoke to us after the game and wished us all the best – he went further actually and told us to go and win it. You appreciate that a lot and it tells you everything you need to know about him as a player and a person. It can't have been easy, but he did it and was a credit to his club.

AnField role models

Y ou do look up to skippers of other teams but the people who you worked under at your own club are probably the most important of all.

Personally, the captains who I've learned from were Jamie Redknapp, Robbie Fowler and Paul Ince.

They were all captains who I worked under full-time as a YTS, a young professional and then when I made the step up to the first team.

There's no better way to lead by example as a captain by hitting the back of the net. It's not about which goal looked the best, or which goal was scored from the longest distance. For me, it's about the importance of the goal and what it means to the football club. Here's eight strikes that bring back some good memories.

8 CAPTAIN'S GOALS

've always been a player who scores in patches. I'll go on a decent run and then go a few games without finding the net.

When I was younger I'd get really worried and uptight about the games where I wasn't scoring. But the more experience I was able to get under my belt the more I realised that if you just keep playing your normal game, take the shots you'd always take, and not try and force the issue then the goals will come.

When I'm not scoring I still have the same number of shots at goal and still get into the same positions. That's something you learn.

Scoring goals in bunches is just the way I am, and probably the way I always will be as a player.

You need a bit of luck to score goals. People forget that but you ask any striker or midfielder and they'll tell you the exact same thing.

Sometimes you get the luck and other times you don't – I've been luckier than most the last few seasons and I've scored some important goals in some important games.

It was a special feeling for me when I went past the 50 goals mark for Liverpool but it didn't last long.

I don't spend a lot of time remembering my first 50 goals or anything else I've helped this team achieve since I made my debut. I'm hungry for the next prize all the time and I'm already chasing 100 goals.

V BOLTON Anfield, Premier League, 01.01.07

I don't normally put too much thought into my celebrations after a goal, normally I just get overtaken by the moment and do what feels right at the time.

Goals are all about helping the team win but a personal one that sticks out in my mind came after I had been announced on the Queen's New Year Honours list.

I scored against Bolton and decided to have a little bit of fun after the ball hit the back of the net.

It was a proud moment for the family and for myself because it's nice to be recognised for what you've achieved on the field of play.

There was a time when I couldn't be sure I'd even get the chance to enjoy a professional career so times like these and moments like that one mean a lot.

But I do know that it wouldn't be happening if it wasn't for the lads here so they are due a debt of thanks too. It's a team game, and I'm fortunate to be part of a great one.

But I'd taken a bit of stick off my mates as you'd expect from a gang of lads from Huyton. There's no chance of your feet ever leaving the ground when you knock about with the boys I knock about with off the field. They were made up I was going to Buckingham Palace to collect an MBE but they weren't going to let the chance to take the mick pass them by.

Anyway, they all sit around the goal-line at the Kop but in the Main Stand. As luck would have it that's where I got the goal that afternoon so I thought I'd give them a special little celebration.

Dirk Kuyt and Jermaine Pennant had tied them in knots on the right wing, creating the space for Dirk to get a cross into the box. I timed my run from the edge of the area and met the ball on the volley from about the penalty spot and it flew past the keeper.

That gave me the chance I'd been looking for so I ran over to the corner where the lads all were and I gave them a little bow!

I ran over to the corner and I gave them a little bow!

My favourite has to be the header in Istanbul

V AC MILAN Atatürk Olympic Stadium, Champions League, 25.05.05

There's no question what my best goal for Liverpool is, in my opinion. As I've already said, it's about the importance of the goal and what it means to the football club.

For that reason my favourite has to be the header I scored in Istanbul to get us back into the game with Milan.

I knew as soon as that left my head it was going into the net but I still watched it carefully just to be sure.

The cross that came into the box was just in the perfect place for me.

There was a bit still to do because Dida's a big keeper but there was plenty of pace still on the ball so it was more about guiding it into the corner.

All I've wanted to do since I was a kid was play for this football club and score goals for this football club.

I've been doing it since I was kicking a ball around the streets and now I can always say I've done it in a Champions League Final.

V OLYMPIAKOS Anfield, Champions League, 08.12.04

You've got to give a lot of credit for that night to the subs and to the manager for making the right alterations at just the right time.

The arrival of Florent Sinama-Pongolle and Neil Mellor changed the game completely. They were two young lads and they came on and did the business for us when we really, really needed it most.

It was just a great night for the club, and that one game gave us a belief and a momentum that we were able to carry all the way to Istanbul.

We didn't play too well in the first half and conceded a silly goal from a free kick, but we kept going and got the right result.

I'd be lying if I said I was always confident we'd do what we needed to do that night. At half time we were losing and we knew the Monaco score. We gave ourselves a mountain to climb but we climbed it and we're all delighted.

Personally, I was delighted to get the winner. Not because of the glory but for the rewards it got the team for the hard work we'd put in on the night – especially in those closing stages.

As the ball dropped towards me it was spinning and I thought the shot was going to end up in the stands when I got my boot to it.

But somehow I caught it sweetly and it flew in.

It's definitely one of the best goals I have ever scored.

I'd be lying if I said I was always confident we'd do it

I don't know if I'd have hit it from there if I'd had more energy

V WEST HAM UNITED Millennium Stadium, FA Cup, 13.05.06

People will probably go on about the second goal in Cardiff but they are both as important as each other.

Both of them were equalisers, both of them kept us in the game. Even though a lot of people remember that game as one of the greatest FA Cup Finals of all time, I still look back on it and think that we should have performed much better than we did.

For long spells of that game we just didn't turn up, and that's not acceptable from a Liverpool team in a final.

But what we did show again that day is that it is impossible to count us out of anything.

As much as everyone goes on about the goal that made it 3-3 I don't know if I'd still have hit it from there if I'd had more energy.

I was dead on my feet and when the ball sat up for me I just thought I'd give it everything I had left.

To be honest I surprised myself with how much I got behind it because I thought the tank was empty.

I like the first goal I scored that afternoon a lot because it was a team goal. I might have put the finishing touch to it but it's a great build-up

that sees Peter Crouch give me a perfect lay-off.

I get more pleasure probably from goals like that than any other kind.

It's like the PFA Player of the Year award I got before the FA Cup Final; it's great to be recognised by my fellow professionals but I was more concerned with the FA Cup trophy and West Ham that weekend.

My target for the season back then was the same as it is before the start of every season – to get to double figures.

As a midfielder I'm always looking to get into double figures, that's the minimum expected of a player in my position.

To get to the next level you're looking at about 15 a season if you want to be classed as a top Premiership midfielder.

If I can get close to 15 a season I'm really happy with that.

The season of the FA Cup was a bit different, I've carried good luck in front of goal and most of my shots have gone in.

That's how I was able to end that season with 23 goals.

But the target every season will be to try and get 15 again.

This goal's right up there with the most important goals I've scored for Liverpool, and it came maybe under the most pressure.

The goals against Olympiakos and West Ham are great moments from the past but I didn't have any time to think about those shots – the ball came to me and I let fly.

This one was different. When I got the ball and placed it on the spot we were heading out of the European Cup and I had this chance to change that.

If I'd missed? I didn't even want to think about that possibility.

I made up my mind where I was putting it as soon as the ref awarded the spot-kick and just concentrated on getting the best contact on the ball that I possibly could. That was enough to put us back in the driving seat and then, as I've already said, Ryan Babel's introduction made sure of our place in the last four.

I made up my mind where to put it

It never
moved. I
caught it
perfectly

V ASTON VILLA Anfield, Premier League, 29.04.06

My second goal in this game was probably the best goal I scored in the 2005/06 season up until we went down to Cardiff for the FA Cup Final.

We'd battered Villa for an hour, taking the lead through Fernando Morientes but then Gareth Barry somehow got them level against the run of play.

We'd worked in training on a corner routine and decided to give it a go with the scores at 1-1. Xabi Alonso drilled one in to the front post and I flicked it into the net.

Then just a few minutes later I tried my luck from distance.

It was one of those shots that I knew had a real chance from the moment that it left my foot and it was great just to stand back and watch it sail into the corner of the net.

I hit it from about 30 yards and it never moved, I just caught it perfectly.

You could probably tell that from my reaction, but I'm not someone who worries generally about how good a goal is.

For me, they all count the same and if it helps us to points and trophies I'm happy – just as I'm happy if I don't score and we still win things.

It's always been a team game to me and that won't ever change.

Personal accolades are things I'll only take stock of when my career's over.

People made us strong favourites against PSV over two legs, but that kind of situation brings with it a different type of pressure.

Sometimes it's an easier situation to be in when you are the underdog.

Looking back at that game I thought the boys coped with the pressure brilliantly.

It was definitely the best away result that we'd posted in the Champions League that season and it gave us a good cushion before they came to Anfield.

We set the tone for the rest of the game in those first five minutes. We were sharp in the tackle and pressed them high up the pitch. We wanted to get at them early, really make life difficult for them and give them doubts because we knew their confidence wouldn't be great after a disappointing month in their league.

Once we had imposed ourselves in the game the football started to flow. That's great credit to our central midfielders who were outnumbered

in that area, but you'd never have known it to look at Javier and Xabi.

When we got the ball down and played the movement was excellent. Every time Steve Finnan crossed the halfway line he looked capable of delivering chances for the forwards and it was the same down the other side where John Arne Riise and Fabio Aurelio worked well.

That stretched the game across the full width of the pitch and created the space that we were eventually able to exploit.

I like this goal for the same reason that my first in Cardiff stands out, it's all about the build-up. Steve Finnan played a brilliant one-two with Javier Mascherano and Finn's actually screaming and pointing to exactly where he wants the return pass played and his cross is perfect.

I'm not the best at the club in the air but I got the forehead on it and opened the scoring. But in terms of the other goals we scored that night in Holland, it was one I could hardly miss.

We made our UEFA Champions League group much more difficult for ourselves than we would have liked at the beginning of last season's competition, but we're absolutely delighted to get through to the last 16 with a cracking win in Marseille.

We were disappointed that it came down to the last game, and that we'd put ourselves in that position in a group that – when the teams were drawn – we thought we'd win if we played to our potential.

We needed a big team performance to get us through, one full of character and hard work.

That's what we got, we were very pleased with how we played that night in the south of France.

The boss talked about that game being a cup final a lot in the build-up to kick-off and it got us really fired up. When he says those two words to us then we know that as players we've got to perform. From Pepe in goal right through the team we did that.

We flew into them from the first whistle. People talk about us being a counter-attacking team and we can play that way if it suits us.

That night in France we took the game to them from the beginning. Maybe they thought we'd invite them on to us but they were mistaken.

They couldn't live with us.

I was fouled for a penalty early on as we ran them all over the place, and they were lucky to keep 11 men on the pitch because it was a last man tackle.

I took the spot-kick and although the keeper saved it the ball broke back to me and I was able to tuck it away at the second attempt.

It wasn't the best goal I've ever scored, but I couldn't care less because it was a game we had to win to progress and it got us off to a good start.

I didn't even know that I had passed Michael Owen's record of 22 goals in Europe until after the game – those are not the kind of thoughts I bother with in the build-up to games as big as that one was.

All that mattered to me in the Stade Velodrome that night was making sure that we were in the draw for the last 16.

FOR CLUB AND COUNTRY

It goes without saying that it's been a tremendous honour to lead England. It's a massive responsibility and I've been extremely proud to have been given the job on a number of occasions.

Doing the double - and Wembley pride

I first captained England less than a year after I had got the full-time job as Liverpool captain. It was a tremendous honour and it meant that I had skippered my club and my country before I'd reached my 24th birthday.

Sweden were the opponents in Gothenburg for a friendly on March 31, 2004 and although the result didn't go our way – we lost 1-0 – it was a special occasion for me.

I only found out that I was going to captain the side the morning before the game. The manager – Sven Goran Eriksson was in charge at the time – pulled me to one side before training and said that he would like me to wear the armband.

As everyone knows, it was a dream come true for myself although it was still a bit of a surprise because there were people in the England squad who were a lot more experienced than me.

So it was a surprise but it was very nice to be captain for one night. I had a bit of a wait before I next wore the England armband. It came almost three years later in another friendly, this time against Spain at Old Trafford.

I have gone on to skipper the national side seven times in all and it's always a tremendous honour. I was also extremely proud to lead out England at the new Wembley.

After wearing the armband for our European Championship qualifier at home to Croatia in November, 2007, new manager Fabio Capello then made me captain for his first game, a friendly against Switzerland in February, 2008.

We had a quick meeting with the new manager when he took over and he told us it was a fresh start for everyone.

He wants a winning mentality around the place, he wants to build a winning team and he wants all the players pulling in the right direction to achieve that. He told us that he's watched us a lot of times and he thinks we can improve defensively and going forward.

When he took over, I said that it would take time because he's a new manager and we don't know much about him and he doesn't know much about us personally. But there's certainly excitement that he's in charge.

He's a very good manager. As a player you want to work with the best and the FA have certainly employed one of the best managers in the world.

'I ONLY FOUND OUT I WAS GOING TO CAPTAIN THE SIDE THE MORNING BEFORE THE GAME. THE MANAGER – SVEN GORAN ERIKSSON WAS IN CHARGE AT THE TIME – PULLED ME TO ONE SIDE BEFORE TRAINING AND SAID THAT HE WOULD LIKE ME TO WEAR THE ARMBAND'

First England armband

v Sweden, aged 23 years 305 days

My story so far

England captain, 2004-2008

March 31, 2004
v SWEDEN (a)
Friendly
Venue: Ullevi, Gothenburg
Result: 0-1

February 7, 2007
v SPAIN (h)
Friendly
Venue: Old Trafford, Manchester
Result: 0-1

October 13, 2007
v ESTONIA (h)
European Championship Qualifier
Venue: Wembley, London
Result: 3-0

October 17, 2007
v RUSSIA (a)
European Championship Qualifier
Venue: Luznikhi, Moscow
Result: 1-2

November 16, 2007
v AUSTRIA (a)
International friendly
Venue: Ernst Happel Stadium, Vienna
Result: 1-0

November 21, 2007
v CROATIA (h)
European Championship Qualifier
Venue: Wembley, London
Result: 2-3

February 6, 2008
v SWITZERLAND (h)
International friendly
Venue: Wembley, London
Result: 2-1

All stats up to and including 16.08.08
Source: englandstats.com

MAGIC OF
THE ARMBAND

*It's the symbol of leadership and the part
of my kit that is most important to me.*

'IT IS AN HONOUR TO WEAR THE ARMBAND AND THAT IS WHY I DON'T THINK IT SHOULD BE PASSED AROUND FREELY'

It's sacred

The captain's armband is very important. It can't be disrespected or passed around too much in a game.

It's easy to pass it around as we've seen in some games but I don't think that should happen.

Every single player wants to be the captain, not just those who are vocal on the pitch, every player. That's how important it is.

You ask any player would they like to captain their club or their country and they will tell you yes.

That applies to any level of the game. Any player who has played the game wants to be a captain.

It is an honour to wear the armband and that is why I don't think it should be passed around freely.

'PLAYERS OFTEN ASK FOR MY SHIRT BUT NOT MANY OPPOSITION SKIPPERS ASK TO SWAP ARMBANDS. JAVIER ZANETTI IS PROBABLY THE BIGGEST OR BEST KNOWN PLAYER WHO HAS ACTUALLY ASKED ME'

Swapping armbands

Players often ask for my shirt but not many opposition skippers ask to swap armbands. Javier Zanetti is probably the biggest or best known player who has actually asked me to swap. He asked me for my armband when we played Inter Milan in the Champions League last season.

I think some captains will do that. A lot of players will ask for shirts for their own collections. I don't really like asking players for their shirts but I do swap a lot of them because people ask me for mine.

But if I can swap a shirt with a decent player it's good because I keep hold of the shirts that I do swap.

You do get a buzz from it sometimes. I've had some top players throughout Europe and the world who have gone out of their way to ask for my shirt.

Even when the game's going on I'll have people asking me to swap afterwards, which is a bit of a problem I've got going on at the moment. It could be when I'm playing teams in the Premier League or wherever and I'll get players distracting me in the middle of a game. It's usually when the game stops for an injury or something and I'll get them coming over asking if we can swap shirts.

If I'm honest though, I do get a kind of buzz out of it because I think 'he really does want my shirt'. Years ago that was me wanting shirts from the players I looked up to. If I got a pair of boots off a Jamie Redknapp, Steve McManaman or a Robbie Fowler I'd be made up. Now it's others asking me so, yes, you do get a buzz sometimes.

'IF WE'VE HAD A BAD DEFEAT OR I DON'T FEEL I'VE PLAYED VERY WELL, I WON'T WEAR THAT ARMBAND...I'LL THROW IT AWAY'

When I change the armband

I can keep the armband between games if I want to but that may depend on results. If we've had a good run of results I don't like to change it.

I can wear the same armband for 10, 12, 15 games if we're doing well.

But the other side of that is if we've had a bad defeat or I don't feel I've played very well.

In those cases I won't wear that armband again. I'll throw it away and get a new one.

The armband is always the last thing I put on before I go out on to the pitch.

Istanbul armband

I might sometimes swap armbands but one I
would never give away is my armband from
Istanbul. That one is special and safely under
lock and key at home!

8 CAPTAIN'S PICTURES

When you're captain of Liverpool Football Club, there's no hiding place from the photographer's lens on the pitch – especially the way the game is now. It's been good to capture some important moments along the way as well as some occasions when your emotions get the better of you. But as they say, the camera never lies.

BACK WHERE HE BELONGS Robbie reunion, Liverpool v Cardiff City, 31.10.07

It was great to see my old mate Robbie Fowler back at Anfield again. I was happy to swap shirts with a Liverpool legend after a hard-fought cup tie with Cardiff.

Disagreeing with Reading's Andre Bikey, Liverpool v Reading 15.03.08

It doesn't matter whether you're captain or not, you are going to have a few disagreements along the way when you're playing in the heart of midfield. This is one occasion when myself and Reading's Andre Bikey came head to head. Let's just say we had a strong exchange of views!

Let's just say we
had a strong
exchange of views!

....he didn't catch me!

Playing a training game with Carra, Melwood, 11.07

Catch me if you can! He didn't – much to the amusement of our team-mates. It's good to mix things up in training and we usually try to do that at Liverpool. These kind of games are always good for team morale, especially if we've got a big match coming up.

Manchester United 0, Liverpool 1 (Murphy) 24.04.04

Danny had a habit of scoring against Manchester United and here we are celebrating the winner in the game at Old Trafford a few years ago. The sun's shining and we got an away victory against one of our greatest rivals – it doesn't get much better than that.

Training with the boss, 11.07

Another lighter moment during the usually serious business of training. This time it's between me and the manager.

Another proud moment for me, captaining England and meeting the dignatories. Prince William also attended training and mixed in well with the lads. We even got Crouchie to do a robot dance for him!

Prince William mixed in well with the lads

END OF THE WORLD After losing the World Club Championships 1-0 to Sao Paolo, Japan, 18.12.05

My expression says it all here – tired and disappointed after a long journey and ultimately defeat.

Tired and disappointed

ANOTHER REUNION Rival captains and friends, Liverpool v Newcastle Utd, Anfield, 08.03.08

Just like with Robbie, here I get to shake hands with an old mate and a Liverpool legend. It felt very strange being on the opposite side of the pitch to Michael after all we've been through.

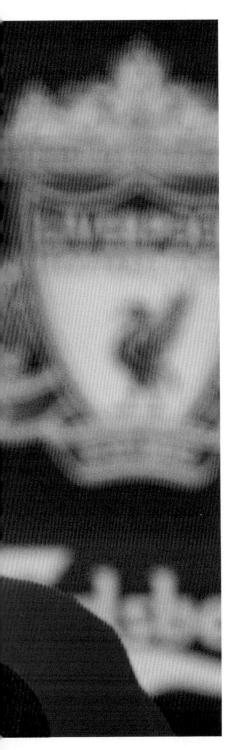

There was a time when I offered to give up the captain's armband of Liverpool. Thankfully the club didn't take me up on the offer. July, 2005 was a nightmare and one which I will never go through again.

GIVING UP THE ARMBAND

In my heart, this is my club. I want to help bring success here for the supporters. For their sake, as well as my own, I never want to go through the events of July, 2005 again.

That was when I told Liverpool that I wanted to leave (to go to Chelsea). But I just didn't want to let go of what I've worked so hard for and as

everyone knows by now, I could never leave this club. I've been here since I was eight years of age. I'd worked hard to become captain and had so many great times and have got great relationships with people here.

I knew the club deserved the next five to 10 years of my career and I didn't – and don't – want to give those years to any other club – I wanted to give them to Liverpool.

Winning the league is what I want more than anything and Liverpool is the only place I have ever wanted to win it.

I think that those few days in early July, 2005, were the most difficult days of my life. I'm not proud of them. I wanted it all to blow over and for it to be forgotten about. I just wanted to get on with my football.

At times, I thought I'd played my last game. I did a lot of thinking and I became really confused.

It was difficult and I wouldn't wish what I went through on any other player or any other person. I know I hurt the fans at the time and they were entitled to their opinion. I had to explain why I was turning down Chelsea at a press conference in June, 2004 – as you can see from these pictures – and I had to put them through it all again a year or so later.

It would have broken my heart

After it all happened, I said to the manager I would like to speak with the players on my own because I knew some of them had been frustrated with what had gone on, just like the fans. I offered to give up the armband which would have broken my heart but I thought it was right to make the offer.

MY DEBT TO OUR 12TH MAN

We've had great times at Anfield in recent seasons. You look back at some of the famous nights here and think of the games against Chelsea, Arsenal, Inter Milan, Juve, and Olympiakos in the Champions League. Then you've got games like Roma, Gerard Houllier's recovery, and the Barcelona game in the treble season.

But you really appreciate our fans sometimes when things aren't going so well. I remember against Benfica in the Champions League in 2005/06. The noise levels when we came out for that game were up there with the very best and the fans stayed with us, urging us on all the way to the end of the game and after the final whistle – even though we ended up going out of the competition.

The one that really stands out for me, though, was the FA Cup third round tie with Arsenal in January, 2007. It didn't go as we wanted, and to be honest, we were gutted to lose to them, for the supporters as much as ourselves. I've never seen anything like that night in my life. The whole place stood for six minutes to make what was a massively important statement to the rest of the country, and to certain individuals.

When the Hillsborough 'Justice' protest ended and the noise was cranked up again it made the hairs on the back of my neck stand up, and it still does now so long after the game.

That level of support and unity is what makes our supporters unique in world football. We've travelled the world playing football and there are some noisy stadiums around – but none comes close to Anfield.

Those supporters are what drives this football club. In that January back in the 2006/07 season, for example, we had a bad week when we went out of both cup competitions but the supporters stayed with us. In the League Cup game – also against Arsenal – they kept willing us forward even though we trailed badly on the scoreboard.

I don't think that there would be too many clubs who at 4-1 down before half-time come out for the second half with the ground still full. It must have been agony for them watching but they stayed with us and helped get us back into the game.

We could feel them willing us forward in the second half and when we got it back to 5-3 the place had a real buzz around it. Unfortunately every time we thought we were getting back at them we gave a goal away again.

It's not just at Anfield where we have a 12th Man. Our fans have followed us all over the world. We all know about the many who made it to Istanbul and Athens but there was even a good showing for the World Club Championship in Japan.

They drive us on for more success, and whenever we are successful, then they will have more than played their part.

Those fans and that attitude will follow us, hopefully, wherever we play.

There's no better group of fans anywhere in the world.

'WHEN THE HILLSBOROUGH 'JUSTICE' PROTEST ENDED AND THE NOISE WAS CRANKED UP AGAIN IT MADE THE HAIRS ON THE BACK OF MY NECK STAND UP, AND IT STILL DOES NOW SO LONG AFTER THE GAME'

'THOSE FANS AND THAT ATTITUDE WILL FOLLOW US, HOPEFULLY, WHEREVER WE PLAY. THERE'S NO BETTER GROUP OF FANS ANYWHERE IN THE WORLD'

Champions of banners

We're renowned as one of the best banner-making clubs in the world and some of our fans have produced some fantastic ones. I've even been the subject of a couple, which gives you a great thrill.

ANFIELD:
THIS IS HOME

*I touch the This Is Anfield sign
when I lead the team out and it's been
my dream to play on the same sacred turf
as so many great players.*

A moving subject

The big stadium move has been a topic on everyone's lips ever since the club announced their plans. In an ideal world, I wouldn't want to move away from Anfield because it's where I used to come to watch Liverpool and it's a ground that has so many happy memories for me as a player too. I've seen and been part of some magical nights there.

It'll be a sad moment for me when the gates close on the old place. The Liverpool supporter in me says I want to stay at Anfield because it's the spiritual home. It's where I came to watch my heroes as a kid and it's where I always dreamed of playing when I was young and kicking a ball about in Huyton.

It's got this sense of history and tradition about it, and I still feel the same walking down and then up the steps on to the pitch as captain today as I did when I made my first start for the team.

I don't care who you are. This stadium, when it's rocking, affects visiting players – every team to play here in Europe said the same.

So with that head on, I'd love us to stay at Anfield, but you've got to look at the bigger picture.

As a player I want to be up there competing for every single trophy we can win. When you look at Chelsea, Arsenal and United they are all pulling more punters into the ground than we are and it makes a difference to our revenue over the season. We're playing catch up every year.

I can see the pros and cons in the move but for financial reasons, and to win things, the time's probably come to go for it.

It will also be a proud moment for me if I get the chance to lead Liverpool into the new era as captain in a new stadium.

That's all we want as players, to be successful long-term. That's what the manager wants and we've got the right man for the job in Rafa. The supporters are used to success and they want more.

We'll be working hard to bring as much of that to Anfield between now and whatever date we move on.

THE CAPTAINS CLUB

I've spoken about how important it is to follow the leaders who have brought such success to Liverpool. It's the ultimate compliment to hear people like former captains Phil Thompson, Alan Hansen and Kenny Dalglish – who also led the team to the Double as manager on the pitch – say nice things about you.

PHIL THOMPSON

'WE KNEW LOOKING AT HIM THAT HE HAD THE TALENT AND THE ABILITY TO GET WHATEVER HE WANTED FROM THIS GREAT GAME. WE ALWAYS BELIEVED HE HAD THOSE TYPE OF LEADERSHIP QUALITIES AND IT'S NO SURPRISE TO ME – OR TO ANYONE AT LIVERPOOL – THAT HE HAS DONE SUCH A GOOD JOB WEARING THE ARMBAND'

I remember talking to Steven in my office at Melwood and trying – as you can in football – to plan his career direction for the future.

I remember telling him that if he made the sacrifices he had to, showed dedication and made the right decisions on, and off, the field then he would go on to captain Liverpool and England.

We knew looking at him that he had the talent and the ability to get whatever he wanted from this great game. We always believed that he had those type of leadership qualities and it's no surprise to me – or to anyone at Liverpool – that he has done such a good job wearing the armband. He's always had it in him and it's no surprise he's gone on to to do the same job for England.

Take Alan Hansen's example. Some people away from Liverpool wondered how he could make a successful captain. That was because he wasn't the most vocal player on the pitch.

But Alan led by example and he inspired with his actions more than his words. He shone as a captain because he showed people the way forward. There was always this great myth that you were a better captain as a central defender because you could see everything that was ahead of you or whatever.

For me, that myth has been laid to rest over the years and if you're a good captain then you're a good captain regardless of your position on the pitch. Steven plays in the middle, in the engine room. When you've got the drive, the determination, the talent and the character that he has on the pitch then you can lead from anywhere on the field.

'STEVEN'S THE KIND OF PLAYER WHO CAN DRIVE TEAMS FORWARD, AND PULL THEM THROUGH GAMES WHEN THEY'RE NOT PLAYING WELL'

It goes back to the point I made earlier about Alan Hansen. Alan was a great captain of our club because he was the best defender in the business at the time and he inspired by example. Other captains make great skippers because they're prepared to bawl and shout at people and make sure they're getting everything from those around them. There are a few types of captaincy in football.

If you look at Steven Gerrard's performances for Liverpool since Gerard Houllier handed him the armband you can see that he's got the ability to lead a team using both those techniques I've just talked about.

When the England captaincy was up for grabs, the southern media, and there are a lot of them, were all pushing John Terry's case. They're perfectly within their rights to do that but Steven Gerrard is a driving force in that team, he's got everything that John Terry's got in terms of motivational skills – but he's just got much, much more in his locker as a football player.

You're not really going to get John Terry popping up with a goal from 35 yards in injury time to carry you across the line the way Stevie can. It's not taking anything away from Terry, but he's a central defender.

There are demands placed on you as Liverpool and England captain in terms of how you live your life and how you behave on and off the park that didn't exist to the same extent when I was a player. There are so many more media outlets now than there were back then and even the paying public have changed somewhat.

They have a desire to know all the ins and outs of professional footballers' lives and the media cater to that but Steven Gerrard has coped with those demands already. He's a family man, a very private person and he's settled down with Alex, had a family – and that all helps you in your football. Things like that help you as a person and as a player. They help you prioritise more than maybe you do when you're a young man about town.

Being captain of Liverpool always offers the obvious chance that you might go on, one day, to captain your country. That was my experience when I was playing as well. It's something that you always long for and hope that it comes your way. Back home in Kirkby and in Liverpool it was a shock to a lot of people but it was such a proud moment for me to be there leading out my country in an international. I was proud as punch coming on to the pitch that day.

With a lot of people, captaining their country is the pinnacle of their career and every time I captained England I was as proud as I was that first time against Bulgaria but I grew up a Liverpool fan and the dream I'd always had was of captaining Liverpool. I'd have to say that captaining Liverpool was the greatest thing in my life in footballing terms.

That doesn't take anything away from the extremely proud moments I had in an England shirt with the captain's armband on. But if you pinned me down I'd still have to say that being captain of Liverpool, a team I'd stood on the Kop so many times supporting, shaded being captain of England.

Steven's the kind of player who can drive teams forward, and pull them through games when they're not playing well.

That's the ability I believe Steven brings to the role of Liverpool skipper.

ALAN HANSEN

'THE BIG THING ABOUT HIM, FOR ME, IS THAT HE ALWAYS PLAYS WITH THE SAME ENTHUSIASM, COMMITMENT AND WILL TO WIN. THAT'S ALL YOU LOOK FOR FROM STEVEN GERRARD. HE'S SUCH A GOOD PLAYER THAT EVERYTHING WILL FALL INTO PLACE IF HE'S GOT THAT ENTHUSIASM'

Steven is a superb captain of Liverpool Football Club. He's the type of leader who inspires his team-mates by performing to the highest standard week in, week out.

The big thing about him, for me, is that he always plays with the same enthusiasm, commitment and will to win.

That's all you look for from Steven Gerrard. He's such a good player that everything will fall into place if he's got that enthusiasm.

He's been moved around from the right to the left but he just gets on with the job.

Steven has been Liverpool's player of the year on a number of occasions and throughout his career, he's just seemed to get better and better, stronger and stronger. Every time he goes out there on the pitch he never says die and that's allied to the quality he's got – and hopefully we haven't seen the best of him yet.

There are a few memorable moments that, for me, sum up what Steven Gerrard means to the Liverpool team and why he leads by example as skipper.

His winning goal against Middlesbrough in the first Premier League home game of the 2008/09 season was fantastic. Every time Liverpool are on the brink of defeat – or dropping points – Stevie can drag them up by the coat-tails.

He did it against Olympiakos when he scored that dramatic late goal to send us through to the Champions League knockout stages in 2005 and then he did it again in the final.

The skipper picked the team up by the bootlaces in the Ataturk Stadium by scoring that first goal and that provided the basis for Liverpool's amazing comeback.

He even ended up at right-back later in the game and was majestic when he played there. Gerrard turned in a performance like you'd never believe that night in Istanbul.

Another big moment that springs to mind for me is the FA Cup final against West Ham in Cardiff. His last gasp equaliser was a monumental hit. He was so far out and the way he hit it and it swerved and bent into the net was unbelievable.

'AS A PLAYER I HONESTLY THINK THAT HE COULD SURPASS KENNY DALGLISH. YOU COULD BE LOOKING AT THE BEST PLAYER TO EVER PULL ON A LIVERPOOL JERSEY. I DON'T SAY THAT LIGHTLY. YOU'VE GOT TO BE EXTRAORDINARILY SPECIAL TO BE BETTER THAN KENNY WAS'

It was a goal out of nothing that only he could have conjured up.

It was the FA Cup final, the 91st minute and there was no way Liverpool were going to score unless he hit one from 40 yards. As soon as he hit it, the goalkeeper knew he had no chance of saving it and Steven's other goal wasn't bad either.

As a player I honestly think that he could go all the way and surpass Kenny Dalglish as Liverpool's greatest ever player. I played alongside Kenny and he did it for 10 years.

If Steven carries on the way he has been then you could be looking at the best player to ever pull on a Liverpool jersey. I don't say that lightly. You've got to be extraordinarily special to be better than Kenny was.

I don't think anyone has come remotely close to being as good as Kenny was until now.

We've seen remarkable performances from him time and time again. The way he drives, leads the team and powers his way through the middle of the park is absolutely exceptional.

That's why it would be fitting if Steven Gerrard was the Liverpool captain who picked up the Premiership trophy. That's what all the supporters want and I know it's what Steven desperately wants.

As I've said, his general enthusiasm is unbelievable and he looks like he's desperate to play for Liverpool and win things. What that can do in the dressing room and on the pitch is carry everyone else up a level. I've seen that before in Liverpool teams of the past. We had characters in there and will to win that you wouldn't find anywhere else and it just brought everyone up a level.

That's what Steven Gerrard does for Liverpool.

KENNY DALGLISH

'IN MY OPINION, STEVEN HAS BEEN ON ANOTHER PLANET TO ANYONE ELSE PLAYING IN HIS POSITION IN THE WORLD'

With Stevie G in the team, anything can and often does happen. In my opinion, Steven has been on another planet to anyone else playing in his position in the world. No-one else offers that versatility, passing range and goals threat from anywhere on the pitch.

It's a proud position being captain of Liverpool but it's also one that brings with it a large degree of pressure and a hell of a lot of responsibility.

Steven handles that and leads by example. When we needed someone in the Ataturk Stadium in 2005 and in the Millennium the year after, it was the captain that came to the rescue of the team.

Another goal springs to mind – in the opening game of the 2007/08 season against Aston Villa. You wondered if it was going to be our day when the ball bounced up and into Carra's hand with five minutes to go but the lads dug in and got a brilliant winner from Stevie.

Liverpool are never a one-man team but he's just so important to us. You cannot overstate the importance of the skipper to this Liverpool team. He's a wonderful talent and a world class player.

Another moment I recall is when he won a penalty against Everton at Goodison. It was classic Steven Gerrard. He left Joleon Lescott for dead at the edge of his own box and then ran away from Tony Hibbert in the Everton half, leaving the Everton right-back with no option but to bring Stevie down.

When he set off from his own area, I don't think too many could see the possibility of anything happening – but Stevie could.

That's why he's the best midfielder in the country.

He sees things first and then acts on them before anyone else has a chance to react.

It's often the case that when he isn't performing miracles, the critics are quick to pounce. It's just typical of the national newspapers. Someone tells a story like Stevie's off the boil and all the others quickly jump on the bandwagon. We'd be in a sorry state with no Stevie G in the team.

He has also struck up quite a partnership with Fernando Torres that I can just see getting better and better.

Stevie and Torres

The combination of Torres and Gerrard on top form is a match for anything in Europe. The way Steven crafts a pass for Fernando is special and, like all good partners, Torres returns the favour. Their understanding is getting on to the telepathic and it's going to be fascinating watching them over the next few seasons.

Torres will learn a lot from playing alongside Stevie and so will the likes of young lads like Lucas. The skipper's influence on those around him just grows and grows.

He wants to lead from the front from the very beginning and if he keeps up his progress, who knows where he might lead us . . .

'HE WANTS TO LEAD FROM THE FRONT FROM THE VERY BEGINNING AND IF HE KEEPS UP HIS PROGRESS, WHO KNOWS WHERE HE MIGHT LEAD US'

MY DEPUTY

It almost goes without saying that I have total respect for Jamie Carragher. Carra is a Liverpool Football Club legend as far as I'm concerned. I was delighted to hand him the armband when he made his 500th appearance for the club last year – he's been a vital part of our success.

Full of guts

I said the year we won the Champions League that Carra had had his best season at the club, and it was going to be tough for him, and the rest of us, to better that achievement in 2005/06 but I was proved wrong.

He went from strength to strength; he was always consistent, he always led by example and he's one of the main reasons why we've been as successful as we have been in the last couple of years.

I'm probably biased because he's one of my mates but he's as good as any defender in Europe. He's not one of those players who only turn it on in big games – you get 100 per cent effort, commitment and dedication from Carra every time he pulls on the Liverpool shirt, it doesn't matter who we're playing.

When I think about how important Jamie's been to us I always think back to Istanbul, he was in agony with cramp but he was still throwing himself into tackles and blocking everything that came his way.

That's Carra – full of guts.

I'm always surprised at how little recognition he gets, he deserves to be in teams of the year and certainly should have been in the running for the PFA awards the last couple of years – but the most important thing is that every person at Liverpool, whether it's the players, manager, back-room staff, board or supporters, know just how important he is to success here.

I hope we've got a lot more to celebrate together in the years to come.

'I'M PROBABLY BIASED BECAUSE HE'S ONE OF MY MATES BUT HE'S AS GOOD AS ANY DEFENDER IN EUROPE'

'HE'S JUST A KID REALLY IN FOOTBALL TERMS AND HE'S GOING TO GET BETTER AND BETTER. THAT'S A FRIGHTENING THOUGHT'

HIS ARMBAND PROVED HE WAS A RED

Kenny talked about the way I've linked up with Fernando and I have to say that he's really added something special to the club. He was a young captain at Atletico Madrid and he's come to Anfield and led our forward line with style. His armband proved he was a Red – and we're happy he's one of us.

World's number one striker

I wouldn't swap him for any striker playing anywhere at the moment. He's been massive for us and gives us so many different things up front.

Obviously because he's a goalscorer that's where he's going to be judged. He's banging them in and always looks a threat every time you play him.

You can play him on his own or with a partner and he just adapts perfectly.

He's made life tough for the foreign boys who come over to England. When you look at the impact he's made in seven months here it means no-one can make excuses about taking time to settle.

I actually think England suits him even better than Spain. He suits the constant flow and rough and tumble of the Premier League better than the stop-start technical La Liga.

He's just a kid really in football terms and he's going to get better and better. That's a frightening thought, not for us but for the defences that are going to come up against him for the next five years – hopefully longer.

THE ARMBAND'S OFF

Every player loves playing football but we all look forward to a break, especially in the summer when the season is over. It's important to recharge the batteries.

Getting away

Usually, after we've played the last match of the season with Liverpool, if I haven't got any England duties, I'll just go to a place where there are a few nice golf courses and a bit of sun and you can put your feet up with your family. The days are long gone where you go to holiday destinations and you go out to nightclubs. You've got to pick a holiday destination where you get your rest and put your feet up otherwise you're not recharging your body in the right way for the forthcoming season.

You can't start playing tennis every day and going running but having said that I think it's important to keep yourself ticking over by walking round golf courses and playing a little bit of tennis every now and then.

You've got swimming in the pool as well but you've got six to eight weeks pre-season training and that's plenty of time to get your fitness back up. It is important that you don't go over the top and put a load of weight on.

Home or abroad?

I definitely go abroad because you can't rely on the weather here. I sometimes have a couple of weeks relaxing in England and then I'll jet off somewhere. Dubai is one of the best places I've been as far as the weather is concerned, things to do and the quality of the place. Everything's quality. It's a very nice holiday and is one of the best places I've been to.

Being recognised

Especially with the international games you play, you do always get recognised wherever you go. Obviously when I'm abroad it's not as much as at home.

Even in the States there are a lot of English tourists who know your face.

Pool or beach?

I prefer the pool rather than the beach to be honest. I'm one of those people who doesn't really like getting sand in my feet. I prefer to chill by the pool with a cold drink.

Take me to the sun

I'm not one of those people who burns or goes red so I'll stick to the low numbers when I'm looking at which factor sun-tan lotion to use. It depends on what mood my wife is in whether or not she'll put it on for me!

Having said that, I have suffered from a little bit of sunburn in the past. If you go from England straight into 80 or 90 degrees then you will suffer but I'm not affected as much as some people.

Speedos or shorts?

I would definitely wear shorts on holiday.

Flip-flops or trainers?

Flip-flops on holiday!

Relaxing between games

I just spend a bit of time with the family and do the usual things in between big games. Sometimes you can quickly forget about what's coming up in the fixture list. Having said that, I can still have the odd restless night when a big match is looming.

Being a Fan

Sometimes the best way to switch off from the pressures of being Liverpool captain is to watch some football. You will often see me supporting the young lads in the Youth Cup. I know how important it is to get encouragement when you're making your way in the game and I have enjoyed watching the teams that Steve Heighway and Gary Ablett have put together. They've had plenty of success in recent seasons. You don't win any trophy without having guts. They've done themselves proud.

Girls fall at my feet!

I get asked to do plenty of things when I'm not playing. One time I was asked by UEFA to be a guest at the Champions League draw in Paris. My appearance was remembered for a different reason . . . when the female presenter fainted in front of me. It was nothing to do with me! I felt really sorry for the girl when it happened because you could see the strain she was under all the way through.

I was told afterwards it was because she hadn't had breakfast, was working in the studio where it was ridiculously hot anyway and she was translating stuff in about three different languages. I'd have fainted too if I'd had to do that.

Some of the lads gave me a bit of stick for not catching her but that's why I'm a midfielder and not a goalkeeper. It's the first time I've had a woman faint at my feet though.

Back to reality

I was asked once if I'd ever sign up to one of the reality TV programmes that are so popular these days. I definitely can't see myself prancing around on skates for Dancing On Ice – I'd get killed by the lads if I ever did that! I don't think I'd be a massive hit in Big Brother either so if I had to pick one, I'd probably say 'I'm A Celebrity . . . Get Me Out Of Here!' because it's a bit harder roughing it in the wild.

IT'S AN HONOUR

Being captain brings other opportunities and responsibilities off the pitch. The most important honours are team honours in my book but it's always a nice bonus to pick up individual awards too.

PFA Player of the Year award

I was in shock, to be honest, when I won this award in 2006. The season before I had come third in the Ballon D'Or behind Ronaldinho and Frank Lampard, but to win this was amazing for me. If you look back at the shortlist, there were five other guys who had so much talent. And then there were also the guys who didn't make the shortlist. There are some fantastic names on the list of past winners – some legends. I was really proud to have joined them, especially when I was told that I was the first Liverpool player to win the award since one of my childhood heroes, John Barnes.

MBE

I t was the perfect end to 2006 when I was told that I was named in the Queen's New Year's Honours List. I was a real thrill to receive an MBE for playing a game I've loved all my life.

We had a fantastic day going down to Buckingham Palace to receive the honour. As I said at the time, I accepted my MBE on behalf of all the people who have been so supportive to me throughout my career, all my team-mates over the years, everyone at Liverpool Football Club and England.

John Moores Honorary Fellowship

Y ou get the chance to do lots of things when you're Liverpool captain and here is me picking up an honorary fellowship from the city's John Moores University during the summer of 2008. As you can see from this picture, I had to don the traditional mortarboard and gown. It was a real honour because not only has LJMU done so much for this city and the people of Liverpool, it has also given the science of football international credibility.

ALWAYS ON MY MIND

Hillsborough service

O ff the pitch, I'm well aware that I have responsibilities on my shoulders as the captain of Liverpool Football Club. Every year, there's one date in my diary that's more important than any other, football or otherwise.

We all go to Anfield every year to pay our respects to the 96 supporters who lost their lives at Hillsborough when they went to watch the Reds in action and didn't return.

It's a difficult time of the year for those families who lost loved ones who went to the match and never returned and it's important we pay our respects and offer our support to the families they've left behind.

Although we pay our respects collectively on the anniversary of the disaster they are never too far from our thoughts.

It's always an afternoon which puts life in real perspective.

"in my own WORDS

A FEW THINGS I'VE SAID IN MY FIVE YEARS AS LIVERPOOL CAPTAIN

"I like being in the dressing room after a good win thinking to myself that I've done my job personally as a player but also that I've done my job as a captain as far as helping people as much as I can"

"I believe I'm a central midfielder but the boss knows that I'll play anywhere for him and this team"

"You don't get any prizes in football for finishing in second place never mind fourth"

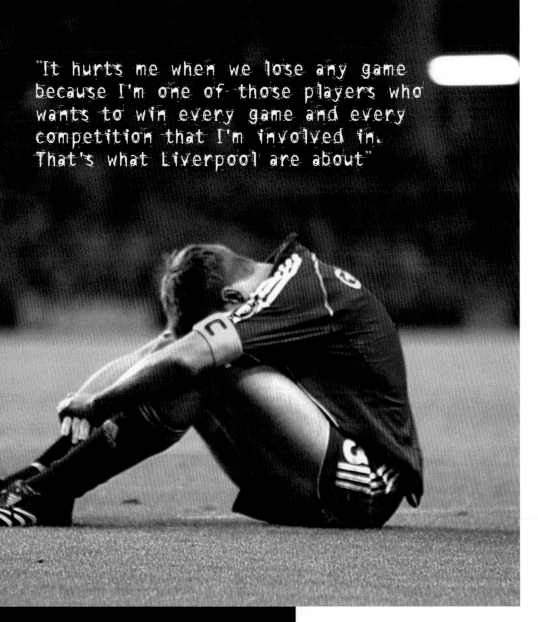

"It hurts me when we lose any game because I'm one of those players who wants to win every game and every competition that I'm involved in. That's what Liverpool are about"

"It's not about one player or even 11 players at this club, we win, lose or draw as a squad"

"It's just the way I was brought up and I suppose where I was brought up. I've never been scared to play against anyone in my life, whether that was in a park in Huyton playing with the older lads or in the final of the European Cup in Athens. The bigger the player, the more that's at stake, the more I like it"

"The derby's a great game. It's the fastest first 20 minutes of any game you'll ever play and then it starts to settle down. Before you know it you're halfway through the first half and you've got a couple of cuts and bruises. They're great to play in"

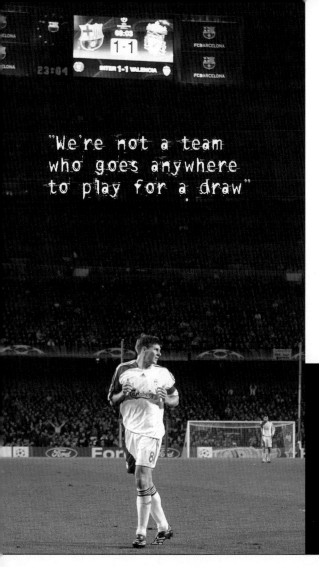

"We're not a team who goes anywhere to play for a draw"

"We shouldn't be relying on the referee to win us games or to change games for us. That's down to us on the field"

"When you're winning games, scoring goals and playing well you're happy to see the games come thick and fast"

"When the fixtures come out at the start of every season the first games you look for as a Liverpool supporter or player are the ones with Everton and Manchester United. They are the biggest games of our season and I don't think you'll find anyone who's not looking forward to them"

"We are everybody's nightmare because we never know when we are beaten and that is a great attitude to have. Even when we don't have an advantage we know we can come back"

"We can beat teams physically and we can beat them with skill and movement. You need both to be successful in this country but you have to get the balance right"

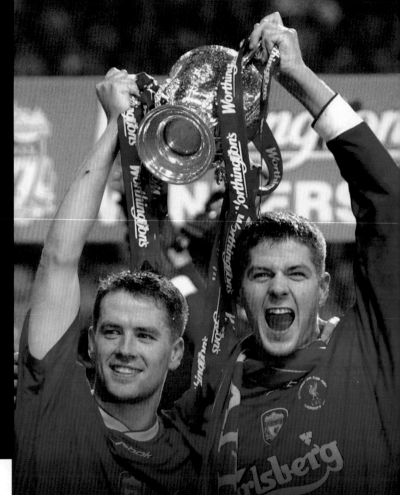

"We don't have preferred trophies here at Liverpool because it's our intention to win everything we compete in. That's just the way it's always got to be at this football club"

"Nothing else is acceptable
other than to be
challenging for honours"

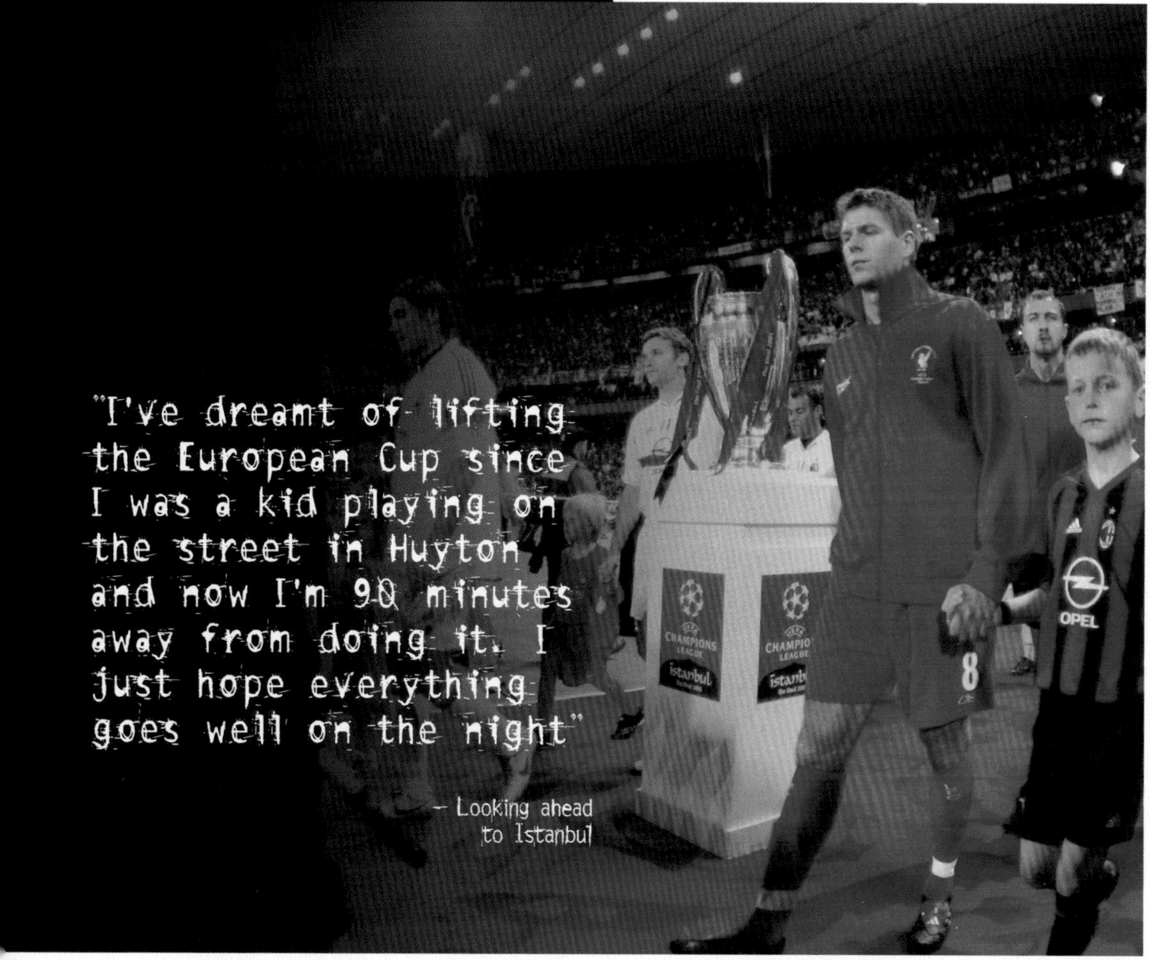

"I've dreamt of lifting
the European Cup since
I was a kid playing on
the street in Huyton
and now I'm 90 minutes
away from doing it. I
just hope everything
goes well on the night"

— Looking ahead
to Istanbul

"I believe you make your own luck,
shape your own destiny..."

HOW MUCH ARE YOU LIKE STEVIE G

**We're coming to the end of the book, so it's time for a bit of fun.
Try and answer these questions and see how much you are like me!**

1. After breaking through into the first team squad the lads give me a nickname. Is it:

a) Gerro.
b) Stevie G.
c) Ged the Red.

2. I'm on the subs bench for the first time in a Merseyside derby when with 19 minutes left to play Gerard Houllier asks me to go on and play at right-back for the injured Vegard Heggem. Do I:

a) Go on and have a shocker by getting myself sent off for a late tackle as Everton go on to win,
b) Go on and score a last minute goal in front of the Kop to give us a 3-2 win.
c) Go on and clear two Everton shots off the goal-line that are celebrated as if I'd scored myself to help us win 3-2.

3. We're at home to Sheffield Wednesday and I've never scored for Liverpool when I get the ball 30 yards from goal. Do I:

a) Unleash an absolute screamer into the top corner to open my account for Liverpool in style.
b) Play a one-two with Karlheinz Riedle on the edge of box before running on to the ball and planting it into the bottom corner.
c) Skip past one defender and power past another into the penalty area before blasting a low shot across the goalie and into the net.

4. I'm playing in the Carling Cup final in Cardiff against Man United when I get the ball 30 yards from goal and decide to shoot. What happens next?

a) The ball hits David Beckham and loops off him over Fabien Barthez and into the net.
b) The ball hits David Beckham in the Goldenballs and he gets carried off on a stretcher.
c) The ball hits David Beckham and bounces straight to Michael Owen who slots it into the net.

5. At the age of 23, Gerard Houllier calls me into his manager's office for a chat. Does he?

a) Tell me he thinks my form has been bad so he's putting me in the reserves for a month.
b) Tell me he thinks I've got the leadership qualities to be the new captain of Liverpool FC and hand me the skipper's armband.
c) Tell me that he can't understand a word Carra says and can I translate for him.

6. At the end of the 2003/04 season what did I do?

a) Go on holiday to the Caribbean with Alex Curran to watch a bit of cricket.
b) Ask if I could have the number 8 shirt instead of 17 now that Emile Heskey has left the club.
c) Get a tattoo of 'Gerrard 8' on my shoulder.

7. Gerard Houllier famously said that if I stay out of nightclubs, one day I'd...

a) Dance as badly as Peter Crouch.
b) Lift the European Cup.
c) Be able to buy one.

8. Reds legend Alan Hansen once described me as "like Graeme Souness with..." What?

a) Pace.
b) Power.
c) No moustache.

9. There are only four minutes left of our final Champions League group match against Olympiakos and unless we score a goal Liverpool are going out. Jamie Carragher launches the ball forward and Neil Mellor heads it into my path 25 yards from goal. Do I?

a) Unleash a stinging drive that rattles off the crossbar and has Sky commentator Andy Gray shouting "unlucky son."
b) Unleash a stinging drive that hits the back of the net and has Sky commentator Andy Gray shouting "take a bow son."
c) Unleash a stinging drive that hits the back of the net and has Sky commentator Andy Gray shouting "you beauty."

10. Liverpool are losing 3-0 in the Champions League final in Istanbul when John Arne Riise's cross comes towards me and I head it into the net. Do I?

a) Run back to the half-way line making a 'come on, we can do this' gesture towards the 40,000 travelling Kopite with my arms.
b) Walk back to the half-way line with a grimace because it's only a consolation and we'll never turn things around.
c) Run at full pelt towards Rafa Benitez and jump into his arms before planting a big kiss on his forehead.

11. I'm about to become the first Liverpool captain to lift the European Cup since Graeme Souness in 1984. As I'm waiting for the trophy to be handed to me do I . . .

a) Plant a kiss on Lennart Johansson.
b) Plant a kiss on Jerzy Dudek.
c) Plant a kiss on the European Cup.

12. When I went to bed after winning the Champions League in Istanbul what did I have in my room?

a) The European Cup.
b) All my mates singing 'Fields of Anfield Road' until 6am.
c) A tourist information leaflet giving directions to the Blue Mosque.

13. According to the song that the Kop sing about me, I can do what?

a) Sweep up my own back yard.
b) Pass the ball 40 yards.
c) Eat half a tonne of lard.

14. In my first game for Liverpool after we had won the Champions League in Istanbul we played TNS. What did I do for the first time for Liverpool?

a) Scored an own goal.
b) Scored a hat-trick.
c) Missed a penalty.

15. When Liverpool won the European Super Cup in 2005 I didn't lift the trophy because?

a) I missed the game through injury so Jamie Carragher was the captain.
b) I'd promised Carra that he could lift the next trophy Liverpool win.

c) Carra ran over and picked it up before I noticed what he was doing.

16. Liverpool are 4-3 up in an FA Cup tie at Luton when Xabi Alonso gets the ball in our half with their goalie out of his net after coming up for a corner. There's one minute left and I've made a lung-busting run into space down the wing when Xabi decides to shoot! Do I:

a) Chase after his shot as quick as I can to see if I can get the final touch before it goes in.
b) Give him a rollicking for not passing it to me before turning round to applaud him when the ball goes in.
c) Stand with my arms aloft as soon as Xabi shoots because he never misses from 60 yards out.

17. We're into injury time in the FA Cup Final against West Ham and although I've scored a goal Liverpool are losing 3-2. With seconds left on the clock I'm in agony with cramp when the ball comes towards me 30 yards from goal. Do I:

a) Knock it back to Jamie Carragher and go down so I can get some attention from the physio for my cramp.
b) Slip a clever pass through for Djibril Cisse who fires home a last-gasp equaliser.
c) Smash the ball goalwards with every ounce of energy I've got and then run towards the Liverpool fans in celebration after it almost rips the net off the frame of the goal.

18. When I scored in the FA Cup Final I became the first ever player to do what?

a) Score in both a League Cup Final and an FA Cup Final for Liverpool.
b) Score in a Champions League Final, UEFA Cup Final, League Cup Final and FA Cup Final.
c) Be the first Scouser to score an FA Cup Final goal for Liverpool.

19. At the end of the 2005/06 season I was voted by my fellow professionals as what?

a) The Most Handsome Footballer of the Year.
b) The PFA Footballer of the Year.
c) European Footballer of the Year.

20. In December 2006 Knowsley Borough Council voted unanimously to make me what?

a) The Lord Mayor of Huyton.
b) An Honorary Freeman of the Borough of Knowsley.
c) Captain of the council's five-a-side team.

21. In which season have I scored the most goals for Liverpool since getting the captain's armband in October, 2003?

a) 2007/08. When I played in a more advanced role behind Fernando Torres.
b) 2005/06. I enjoyed a great campaign and scored twice in the FA Cup Final.
c) 2004/05. In the season that we won the Champions League.

22. When I opened the scoring in Liverpool's must-win Champions League match in Marseille in December 2007 I set a club record for what?

a) Most goals scored in European competition by

a Liverpool player.
b) Most goals scored by a Liverpool player in France.
c) Most goals scored in the same season in the Champions League.

23. Fernando Torres and I have formed a superb partnership together that has seen us compared to which famous other Liverpool duo?

a) Toshack and Keegan.
b) Rush and Dalglish.
c) Lennon and McCartney.

24. Liverpool are going out of the Champions League in the quarter-final against Arsenal at Anfield when Ryan Babel wins a penalty with just four minutes left. Do I:

a) Slam the ball high to Manuel Almunia's right and into the net to send Anfield wild with joy.
b) Slot the ball low to Manuel Almunia's left and into the net to send Anfield wild with joy.
c) Smack the ball right down the middle past Manuel Almunia to send Anfield wild with joy.

25. Next season if I could lift just one trophy which one would it be?

a) The Champions League
b) The FA Cup
c) The Premier League

How did you score?

1. a)2 b)5 c)1, **2.** a)1 b)2 c)5, **3.** a)2 b)1 c)5,
4. a)5 b)1 c)2, **5.** a)1 b)5 c)2, **6.** a)1 b)5 c)2
7. a)1 b)2 c)5, **8.** a)5 b)2 c)1, **9.** a)1 b)2 c)5
10. a)5 b)2 c)1, **11.** a)1 b)2 c)5, **12.** a)5 b)2 c)1
13. a)2 b)5 c)1, **14.** a)1 b)5 c)2, **15.** a)5 b)2 c)1
16. a)1 b)5 c)2, **17.** a)1 b)2 c)5, **18.** a)2 b)5 c)1
19. a)1 b)5 c)2, **20.** a)2 b)5 c)1, **21.** a)1 b)5 c)2
22. a)5 b)1 c)2, **23.** a)2 b)5 c)1, **24.** a)5 b)1 c)2
25. a)2 b)1 c)5

If you scored...25-50

Are you sure you're a Steven Gerrard fan? Judging by those answers it appears you either know nothing about me or you're a Man United fan! You need to swot up on your Liverpool facts if you want to start thinking like I do or else people will start to think that you prefer Rio Ferdinand!

If you scored...51-100

Not a bad effort but you could've done better. You clearly know a thing or two about me but if you want to truly think like I do then there is still room for improvement. A bit of extra work with Rafa and the boys on the training ground should do it.

If you scored...100-125

Not only do you know all about me, you also think like you're the Liverpool skipper. Your knowledge is first class and you should really go on Mastermind and pick Stevie G as your specialist chosen subject. Next time I'm injured, you can wear the armband. Well done!

STEVEN GERRARD: STATISTICS

Liverpool career statistics as captain (up to start of the 2008/09 season)

Season	Appearances	Goals
2003/04	39	6
2004/05	43	13
2005/06	53	23
2006/07	51	11
2007/08	52	21

Liverpool career statistics BEFORE he was captain

Season	Appearances	Goals
1998/99	13	0
1999/00	31	1
2000/01	50	10
2001/02	45	4
2002/03	54	7
2003/04	8	0

(Gerrard's first official game as Liverpool skipper was October 15, 2003 v Olimpija Ljubljana)

Steven Gerrard's goals since being appointed as Liverpool skipper.
(In total Stevie has scored 96 goals for the club, 74 of them since he's worn the captain's armband and 68 of them under the management of Rafa Benitez)

1) 30/11/03	Birmingham	H	Premier League	WON 3-1
2) 07/02/04	Bolton	A	Premier League	DREW 2-2
3) 11/02/04	Man City	H	Premier League	WON 2-1
4) 26/02/04	Levski Sofia	H	UEFA Cup	WON 2-0
5) 03/03/04	Levski Sofia	A	UEFA Cup	WON 4-2
6) 08/05/04	Birmingham	A	Premier League	WON 3-0
7) 10/08/04	Graz AK	A	Champions League	WON 2-0
8) 10/08/04	Graz AK	A	Champions League	WON 2-0
9) 21/08/04	Man City	H	Premier League	WON 2-1
10) 11/09/04	West Brom	H	Premier League	WON 3-0
11) 08/12/04	Olympiacos	A	Champions League	DREW 2-2
12) 14/12/04	Portsmouth	H	Premier League	DREW 1-1
13) 26/12/04	West Brom	A	Premier League	WON 5-0
14) 11/01/05	Watford	H	League Cup	WON 1-0
15) 25/01/05	Watford	A	League Cup	WON 1-0
16) 20/03/05	Everton	H	Premier League	WON 2-1
17) 30/04/05	Middlesbrough	H	Premier League	DREW 1-1
18) 08/05/05	Arsenal	A	Premier League	LOST 1-3
19) 25/05/05	AC Milan	N	Champions League	DREW 3-3*
20) 13/07/05	TNS	H	Champions League	WON 3-0
21) 13/07/05	TNS	H	Champions League	WON 3-0
22) 13/07/05	TNS	H	Champions League	WON 3-0
23) 19/07/05	TNS	A	Champions League	WON 3-0
24) 19/07/05	TNS	A	Champions League	WON 3-0
25) 27/07/05	FBK Kaunas	A	Champions League	WON 3-1
26) 02/08/05	FBK Kaunas	H	Champions League	WON 3-1
27) 02/10/05	Chelsea	H	Premier League	LOST 1-4
28) 25/10/05	Crystal Palace	A	League Cup	LOST 1-2
29) 05/11/05	Aston Villa	A	Premier League	WON 2-0
30) 30/11/05	Sunderland	A	Premier League	WON 2-0
31) 15/12/05	Deportivo Saprissa	N	World Club Challenge	WON 3-0
32) 26/12/05	Newcastle	H	Premier League	WON 2-0
33) 28/12/05	Everton	A	Premier League	WON 3-1
34) 02/01/06	Bolton	A	Premier League	DREW 2-2
35) 07/01/06	Luton	A	FA Cup	WON 5-3
36) 29/01/06	Portsmouth	A	FA Cup	WON 2-1
37) 01/02/06	Birmingham	H	Premier League	DREW 1-1
38) 19/03/06	Newcastle	A	Premier League	WON 3-1
39) 29/04/06	Aston Villa	H	Premier League	WON 3-1
40) 29/04/06	Aston Villa	H	Premier League	WON 3-1
41) 13/05/06	West Ham	N	FA Cup	DREW 3-3*
42) 13/05/06	West Ham	N	FA Cup	DREW 3-3*
43) 31/10/06	Bordeaux	H	Champions League	WON 3-0
44) 22/11/06	PSV Eindhoven	H	Champions League	WON 2-0
45) 25/11/06	Man City	H	Premier League	WON 1-0

46) 09/12/06	Fulham	H	Premier League	WON 4-0
47) 16/12/06	Charlton	A	Premier League	WON 3-0
48) 01/01/07	Bolton	H	Premier League	WON 3-0
49) 09/01/07	Arsenal	H	League Cup	LOST 3-6
50) 24/02/07	Sheffield United	H	Premier League	WON 4-0
51) 03/04/07	PSV Eindhoven	A	Champions League	WON 3-0
52) 18/04/07	Middlesbrough	H	Premier League	WON 2-0
53) 18/04/07	Middlesbrough	H	Premier League	WON 2-0
54) 11/08/07	Aston Villa	A	Premier League	WON 2-1
55) 24/10/07	Besiktas	A	Champions League	LOST 1-2
56) 28/10/07	Arsenal	H	Premier League	DREW 1-1
57) 31/10/07	Cardiff	H	League Cup	WON 2-1
58) 06/11/07	Besiktas	H	Champions League	WON 8-0
59) 10/11/07	Fulham	H	Premier League	WON 2-0
60) 24/11/07	Newcastle	A	Premier League	WON 3-0
61) 28/11/07	Porto	H	Champions League	WON 4-1
62) 02/12/07	Bolton	H	Premier League	WON 4-0
63) 08/12/07	Reading	A	Premier League	LOST 1-3
64) 11/12/07	Marseille	A	Champions League	WON 4-0
65) 26/12/07	Derby	A	Premier League	WON 2-1
66) 15/01/08	Luton	H	FA Cup	WON 5-0
67) 15/01/08	Luton	H	FA Cup	WON 5-0
68) 15/01/08	Luton	H	FA Cup	WON 5-0
69) 02/02/08	Sunderland	H	Premier League	WON 3-0
70) 19/02/08	Inter Milan	H	Champions League	WON 2-1
71) 05/03/08	West Ham	H	Premier League	WON 4-0
72) 08/03/08	Newcastle	H	Premier League	WON 3-0
73) 08/05/08	Arsenal	H	Champions League	WON 4-2
74) 13/04/08	Blackburn	H	Premier League	WON 3-1

*Liverpool won on penalties

Compiled by Chris McLoughlin

Complete Liverpool captains (taken from www.lfchistory.net)

Name	Period	Trophies won
Andrew Hannah	1892-95	
Jimmy Ross	1895-97	
John McCartney	1897-98	
Harry Storer	1898-99	
Alex Raisbeck	1899-1909	2 leagues
Arthur Goddard	1909-12	
Ephraim Longworth	1912-13	
Harry Lowe	1913-15	
Ephraim Longworth/Don MacKinlay	1919-20	
Ephraim Longworth	1920-21	
Don MacKinlay	1921-28	2 leagues
Tom Bromilow	1928-29	
James Jackson	1929-30	
Tom Morrison	1930-31	
Tom Bradshaw	1931-34	
Ernie Blenkinsop/Tom Cooper	1934-35	

Ernie Blenkinsop	1935-36	
Ernie Blenkinsop/Tom Cooper	1936-37	
Tom Cooper	1937-39	
Matt Busby	1939-40	
Willie Fagan	1945-47	1 league
Jack Balmer	1947-50	
Phil Taylor	1950-53	
Bill Jones	1953-54	
Laurie Hughes	1954-55	
Billy Liddell	1955-58	
Johny Wheeler	1958-59	
Ronnie Moran	1959-60	
Dick White	1960-61	
Ron Yeats	1961-70	2 leagues, 1 FA Cup
Tommy Smith	1970-73	1 league, 1 UEFA Cup
Emlyn Hughes	1973-78	2 leagues, 2 European Cups, 1 UEFA Cup, 1 FA Cup, 1 European Super Cup
Kenny Dalglish	1978-78	
Phil Thompson	1979-81	2 leagues, 1 European Cup, 1 League Cup
Graeme Souness	1982-84	3 leagues, 1 European Cup, 3 League Cups
Phil Neal	1984-85	
Alan Hansen	1985-88	2 leagues, 1 FA Cup
Ronnie Whelan	1988-89	1 FA Cup
Alan Hansen	1989-90	1 league
Ronnie Whelan	1990-91	
Steve Nicol	1990-91	
Mark Wright	1991-93	1 FA Cup
Ian Rush	1993-96	1 League Cup
John Barnes	1996-97	
Paul Ince	1997-99	
Jamie Redknapp	1999-2002	1 UEFA Cup, 1 FA Cup, 1 League Cup, 1 European Super Cup
Sami Hyypia	2001-03	1 League Cup
Steven Gerrard	**2003-present**	**1 European Cup, 1 FA Cup, 1 European Super Cup**

(The 'trophies won' section lists the trophies that Liverpool won during that player's time as club captain, irrespective of whether the individual played in or missed the game when a trophy was won. For instance, Jamie Redknapp missed the entire 2000/01 season through injury but was the club captain at the time of the cup treble. Some of the names listed were appointed as captains on a temporary basis while the normal skipper was injured such as Ronnie Whelan in 1988/89.)

I'D PREFER TO RETIRE THE ARMBAND RATHER THAN SOMEONE COME TO ME AND SAY 'YOU'RE NOT CAPTAIN ANYMORE' ... I'VE STILL GOT BIG AMBITIONS

No plans to retire

I totally respect the way Sami was with me when I was first given the armband and I have learned that's the way I would expect to react myself if the captaincy is ever taken off me.

Hopefully it doesn't ever come to that.

I'd prefer to retire the armband rather than someone come to me and say 'you're not the captain anymore – this kid or whoever is taking over'.

I'd rather it be at the beginning of a season, if I feel my legs are going or something, or if I've become more of a squad player.

Then I'd rather hand it over myself.

But I've still got big ambitions as captain of Liverpool Football Club. There's a lot I still have to learn and a lot I want to achieve. It's far from over.

I was wearing the yellow Champions League armband when we won in Istanbul.

Winning the Champions League has to be the biggest thing that has happened to me in football so far. To lift the title while wearing the Premier League captain's armband would have to be up there with Istanbul without a shadow of a doubt.

It's the same buzz for me whether I've got a Premier League or Champions League armband on. It makes no difference.

'THE TITLE HAS BEEN TOO LONG AWAY FROM ANFIELD AND WE'RE DETERMINED TO START ANOTHER LEGACY HERE IN OUR TIME'

It's not like I go out and give 70-80 per cent in the Carling Cup and 80-90 per cent in the FA Cup. I give it 100 per cent every time I put that armband on.

I got the same buzz out of lifting the FA Cup as I did lifting the Champions League trophy. I know the Champions League is on a much bigger scale than the FA Cup and if I had to pick one I'd go for the Champions League.

But I still got that buzz and the same feelings through my body when I lifted those two cups as captain of this club.

I'm sure I'll experience the same if not more when we win the Premier League.

I'm confident it's going to come.

We might have to be patient but I've got confidence it'll happen.

I grew up watching Liverpool teams, great teams with great players, winning title after title and you just expected that dynasty to continue.

It's been too long away from Anfield and we're determined to start another legacy here in our time.

We feel we've got the players here to do that.